CONTENTS

ARGENTINA TODAY

ARGENTINA IS THE WORLD'S EIGHTH-LARGEST COUNTRY AND the second-largest country in South America. It is the size of Alaska, Texas, California, and Alabama combined and is a recognized middle power—a country with moderate influence in the international arena. Argentina is one of South America's largest economies, with a high quality of life and gross domestic product (GDP) per capita. The GDP is a measure of the goods and services produced in a country. The people of Argentina are recovering from a tumultuous economic history and horrifying inflation, and today the Argentines are deservedly proud of their country with its colorful history and unique peoples.

Any visitor to Argentina would be amazed by its breathtaking geography, its mountain peaks, sandy beaches, and fertile plains. The name Argentina comes from the Latin word *Argentum*, which means "silver." The origin of the name goes back to the indigenous people who gave silver objects to the Spanish conquerors as gifts and the news about a legendary mountain rich in silver that reached Spain about 1524.

Cacti and small shrubs thrive in the dry landscape of Los Cardones National Park.

Geographically the country has an enormous contrast among its four varied parts:

- the immense eastern plains of the Pampas, the source of agricultural wealth in Argentina and the land of the gauchos—South American cowboys—which includes the province of Buenos Aires, south of Córdoba, and south of Santa Fe;
- the impressive Andes mountain range along the western border separating Argentina from Chile, where the highest peaks in South America stand;
- toward the south where the sterile and stony but oil-rich plateaus of Patagonia appear;
- the subtropical area of the Chaco to the north, with forests, scrubland, and wetlands, home to a large number of vegetal and animal species. The province of Santiago del Estero belongs to the drier part of the Gran Chaco.

Argentina's territory has great climatic variety. In the north it is subtropical, in south Patagonia it is subantarctic, and in the Pampas the climate is mild and humid. Argentina's population is 41.8 million. The official language is Spanish (some *lunfardo* [slang] expressions are used too), but English, Italian, German, and French are also spoken. The official religion is Roman Catholic, but there is absolute religious freedom in Argentina.

The official Argentine currency is the *peso*. There are bills of 2, 5, 10, 20, 50, and 100 pesos and coins of 1 peso and 1, 5, 10, 25, and 50 cents, although you can choose to pay using U.S. dollars, credit and debit cards, or traveler's checks.

TOURIST ATTRACTIONS

BUENOS AIRES   Buenos Aires is the most European-looking capital city in South America. *Porteños* (locals) are very friendly and have a rich and diversified cultural identity. There is a lot to see here. Visitors could go to one of many classical attractions:

- La Boca, with its colorful houses and restaurants;
- San Telmo, with its tango shows in Plaza Dorrego on Sundays;
- the Cementerio de la Recoleta, where the remains of Eva Perón are buried in the Duarte family tomb;
- the Plaza de Mayo, where several of the city's major landmarks are located: the Cabildo (the city council during the colonial era), the Casa Rosada (home of the executive branch of the federal government), the Metropolitan Cathedral of Buenos Aires, the May Pyramid, and the current city hall or *municipalidad*;
- Palermo, where the Museum of Art of Buenos Aires and the Buenos Aires Zoo are located;
- the shopping areas in Belgrano.

IGUAZÚ WATERFALLS   The falls are the result of a volcanic eruption, which left a large crack in the Earth. They are located at the border of Argentina, Brazil, and Paraguay. They have been designated as a United Nations Educational, Scientific and Cultural Organization (UNESCO) World Natural Heritage Site. Near Iguazú there are other important attractions, such as the Jesuit missions of the Guaraníes and the Itaipú hydroelectric power plant.

EL CALAFATE   El Calafate is a peaceful and picturesque village, where the beauty of Patagonia can be discovered. Its name comes from the calafate, a thorny shrub with yellow flowers and dark blue berries, which is found over the whole region of Patagonia. The city of Calafate is the hub to visit the famous Perito Moreno glacier in Los Glaciares National Park.

The Piramide de Mayo obelisk at Plaza de Mayo is one of the most famous landmarks of Buenos Aires.

CATAMARCA The province of Catamarca is located in the northwest of Argentina. Catamarca is chosen by tourists from all over the world for its attractive landscapes, cultural places, and ecological areas where activities such as mountain bike rides, hiking, and horseback riding are offered. The rivers are rich with trout and the view from the mountains is breathtaking.

SANTIAGO DEL ESTERO Santiago del Estero, founded in 1553, is the oldest city in the country. Its Basilica Cathedral, erected in 1570, was the first to be built in Argentina. It is located on the banks of Río Dulce (Sweet River) and is a distance of 647.5 miles (1,042 kilometers) from Buenos Aires. Interesting places in the city include the Universidad Nacional de Santiago del Estero, founded in 1973; the Universidad Católica, founded in 1960; the Santo Domingo Convent, and the Provincial Archaeology Museum.

Happy harvesters during a merlot harvest at Bodegas Salentein vineyard in Mendoza.

WINE TOURISM IN MENDOZA Mendoza in northwestern Argentina is the place to enjoy Argentine wines. Many bodegas (wineries) offer wine tasting for free. There are numerous famous local wine varieties, especially the red Malbec and the white Torrentes. One way to visit the numerous bodegas is by bike. The tourist can enjoy the landscape, the beautiful vineyards, and sample wines all day.

EL VALLE DE LA LUNA This is a national park in the San Juan province of Argentina. It is the best place for paleontological tourism because it contains some of the oldest known dinosaur remains, dating back millions of years. At this UNESCO World Heritage site, tourists can see some gray-green rocks that have eroded into strange formations. Today they are known as Aladdin's Lamp, The Parrot, and The Mushroom. The valley is sparsely populated by pumas, guanacos, condors, and the South American ostrich.

PUERTO MADRYN This is the gateway to the Península Valdés, a wildlife sanctuary for birds and marine species where visitors can watch varied and important sea fauna such as the cormorant, egret, flamingo, whales, Magellanic penguins, oyster-catchers, petrels, rheas, sea elephants, sea lions, and many other species of wildlife. With more than 18 miles (30 km) of beaches with crystal-clear water, the city is a popular destination for wildlife excursions and sports such as mountain biking, windsurfing, fishing tournaments, snorkeling, jet skiing, water skiing, sailing, and scuba diving. This is the Argentine capital of subaquatic activities.

The Tren de las Nubes train passing through La Polvorilla viaduct in Salta.

EL TREN DE LAS NUBES Riding the famous Tren de las Nubes (Train to the Clouds), passengers will travel the third-highest railway in the world, reaching almost 13,123 feet (4,000 meters) above sea level. During the 135-mile (217-km) journey, visitors will feel as if they are hanging from the clouds because clouds can often be seen around and under the bridges through the railway passes. The Tren de las Nubes leaves once a week from Salta (which is 3,881 feet, or 1,183 m, above sea level) and travels 270 miles (434 km) to the La Polvorilla viaduct (which is 13,845 feet, or 4,220 m, above sea level), utilizing the General Belgrano railroad. The route has 19 bridges, 21 tunnels, 13 viaducts, 2 spirals, and 2 zigzags. The convoy of 10 wagons can carry 640 passengers at an average speed of 21.75 miles per hour (35 km/hour). The train has a buffet car, an onboard medic, and audio and video facilities.

ARGENTINE FOOD

Argentine cuisine has been influenced heavily by European cuisine, especially Italian, Spanish, and French. Argentina is one of the major food producers of the world. It is a leading producer of beans, corn, meat, milk, wheat, and soybeans. Therefore red meat, pastas, and white bread (made with wheat flour) form a huge part of the Argentine diet.

A traditional Patagonian meal consisting of mate, beer, and *locro*.

Milanesas are a favorite meat dish made up of beef, chicken, or veal and beaten eggs seasoned with paprika, salt, and other ingredients. Pastries of meat, cheese, and sandwiches are common as well. Argentineans also eat lots of vegetables and salads.

In Argentina beef is of the highest quality. In Patagonia lamb and goat are more common than beef. *Chimichurri*, a seasoning of herbs and chili, is often the only sauce for steak and chorizo.

There are plenty of Italian staples, including cannelloni, gnocchi, pastas, pizza, and ravioli, which can be bought in the different markets of Argentina.

Other popular foods include the tasty stew *puchero*, *locro* (a pork and corn stew), sweet squash in cream, *tartas* (pie), empanadas (puff pastry stuffed with different ingredients, usually meat), and *dulce de leche (DOOL-seh de LAy-cheh)*. A national obsession, *dulce de leche*, a thick, caramel-like, milk-based sauce or spread, can be found in all corners of the country. It is used to fill cakes and pancakes and is spread over toasted bread. *Alfajores* are shortbread cookies filled with *dulce de leche* and coated in chocolate, and *panqueques* are delicious crepe desserts. The "policeman's" or "truck driver's" sweet cheese with quince paste, or *dulce de membrillo*, is yet another favorite food. It is so named because the cop can eat it standing up and can wolf it down if he has to leave for an emergency.

The people of Argentina like wine and beer to go with their meals. Argentine wines are excellent. Local distilleries produce their own beer. "Quilmes" is the national brand of lager.

The national drink of Argentina is an infusion called mate. At family or social gatherings, the drinking of mate is seen as an important social ritual, with the host preparing the beverage according to each guest's preference.

FESTIVALS OF ARGENTINA

THE GUALEGUAYCHU CARNIVAL The Gualeguaychu Carnival is one of the biggest carnivals in Argentina, where *comparsas* (groups of people dancing to happy music and dressed in colorful suits), *murgas* (bands of street musicians), and other artists participate in giant parades or *corsos* along the streets. This carnival takes place in the province of Entre Rios during January and February. It is marked by music, folk dances, water fights, and a local brew called *chicha*.

BUENOS AIRES TANGO FESTIVAL This festival has been celebrated since 1999. It happens between February and March and is organized by the Argentine Ministry of Culture. There are free tango classes and tango performances by celebrated dancers across the city, as well as parties.

Musicians performing with traditional Argentine instruments in Buenos Aires.

IMMIGRANTS' FESTIVAL The Immigrants' Festival is celebrated in the city of Oberá, the province of Misiones, Argentina, during the first two weeks in September in the Parque de las Naciones (Nations' Park). The different communities, called *colectividades* (collectives), show their different customs through dance, food, clothing, and related activities.

OKTOBERFEST ARGENTINA Since 1964 thousands of people have been arriving in Villa General Belgrano, Córdoba, to take part in the German celebration called Oktoberfest. Over the course of five days each person participating in this festival drinks more than a gallon of beer. The main beer trademarks take part in this celebration. This festival is acclaimed as the third most important Oktoberfest site in the world, after Munich in Germany and Blumenau in Brazil.

CREAMFIELDS BUENOS AIRES This large dance music festival is celebrated every year in November in the 32-acre (13-hectare) old Boca Juniors football ground in the Costanera Sur area of the city.

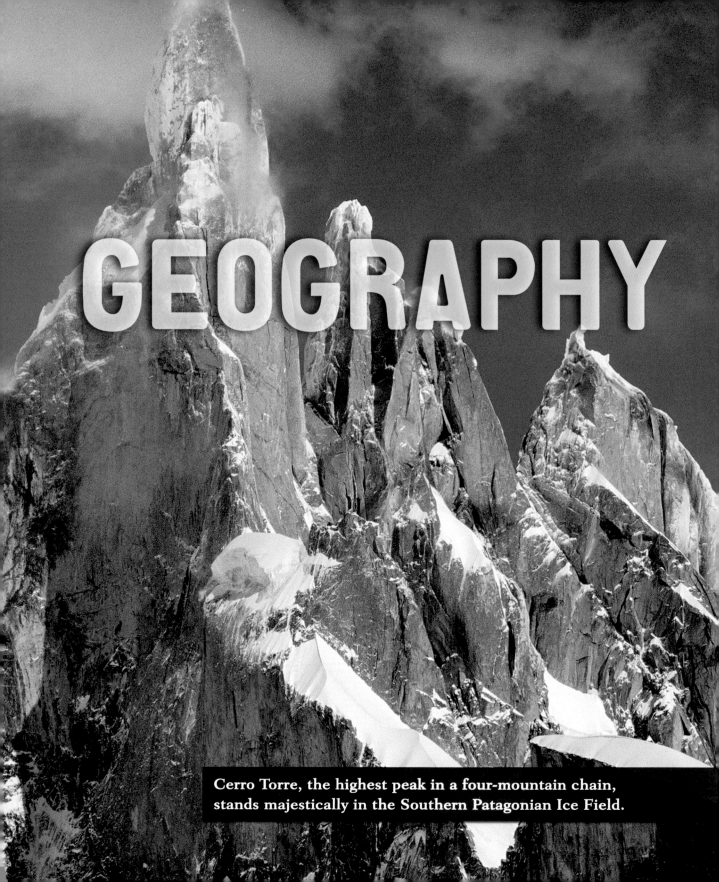

GEOGRAPHY

Cerro Torre, the highest peak in a four-mountain chain, stands majestically in the Southern Patagonian Ice Field.

WHETHER YOU DREAM OF mountain peaks, sandy beaches, or fertile plains, Argentina has them all. This vast South American country stretches about 2,400 miles (3,900 km) long and has a dramatically diverse climate, ranging from subtropical in the north to subantarctic in the south.

Because Argentina lies in the Southern Hemisphere, the climate is hottest in the north, near the equator, and coldest in the south.

LANDSCAPE

Argentina is the eighth-largest country in the world and the second-largest country in South America, after Brazil. Argentina's landmass covers almost 1.1 million square miles (2.8 million square km) and measures 868 miles (1,397 km) across at its broadest point.

Argentina's neighbors are Bolivia and Paraguay to the north, Brazil and Uruguay to the east, and Chile to the south and west. The Atlantic Ocean on the east and south and the Andes Mountains to the west form long natural borders.

Argentines are proud of their country's great natural beauty. Featuring long stretches of snowcapped mountains and miles of seashore, Argentina boasts remarkable extremes in elevation. The Laguna del Carbon in Santa Cruz Province is 344 feet (105 m) below sea level. Near the Chilean border, the summit of Mount Aconcagua, an extinct volcano, is the highest peak in the Western Hemisphere—22,834 feet (6,960 m) high.

1

The Argentine Republic is located in the Southern and Western hemispheres. Its relative position in South America gives the country a huge diversity of land and culture.

THE NORTHERN LOWLANDS

Northern Argentina consists of heavily forested lowlands. The early settlers called one area in this region the Gran Chaco, or hunting ground, to distinguish it from the Pampas, a vast cattle-grazing region farther south.

Few people live in the forests of the Chaco. The region is rich in forest products, but its fertility is limited in some parts by swamps and in other parts by periodic drought. Winters are dry, whereas summers are hot and humid, with temperatures rising as high as 117°F (47°C).

Another area in the northern lowlands is called Mesopotamia, and it includes the provinces of Entre Ríos, Corrientes, and Misiones. Both *Mesopotamia* and *Entre Ríos* mean "between rivers." This area lies between the Paraná and Uruguay rivers. Rolling grassy plains, rivers, and swamps are the chief features. The climate is warm and wet all year-round. Ranchers raise cattle, horses, and sheep; farmers grow flax, wheat, and fruits.

The Misiones province in northeastern Mesopotamia has heavy rainfall and thick forests. The spectacular Iguazú Falls on the Brazilian border are also located here. The region's most famous crop is the holly plant, used to make yerba mate. This brewed herbal tea, the gaucho's favorite drink, is served all over Argentina.

THE PAMPAS

More than two-thirds of Argentina's population lives in the Pampas. The nation's main economic activities are centered in this region. The capital, Buenos Aires, is located here. Most big cities, industries, and important transportation facilities are also found in this part of the country.

The Pampas are flat and fertile plains with a temperate climate. They stretch over the central part of the country from the Atlantic Ocean to the Andes Mountains. The Pampas cover one-fifth of Argentina's land area.

The word *Pampas* comes from a Guaraní Indian word meaning "level land." Visitors to Argentina are often astounded when they see the Pampas stretching to the horizon in all directions, with barely a tree or rock to catch the eye, and looking as flat as the sea. Many of the country's chief crops—

IGUAZÚ FALLS: A WORLD-CLASS TOURIST DESTINATION

Misiones, in northeastern Mesopotamia, boasts many spectacular waterfalls. The impressive Iguazú Falls on the Brazilian border is the most awesome of them all. Álvar Núñez Cabeza de Vaca, a Spaniard, explored this gorgeous cascade in 1541.

Iguazú is a Guaraní Indian word meaning "great water." More than 275 waterfalls surround an 8,100-foot-wide (2,469-m-wide) arc in the Iguazú River. These waterfalls plunge roughly 270 feet (82 m) over a series of small islets, creating spectacular sprays and rainbows. The largest waterfall, called Devil's Throat, is more than 350 feet (107 m) high.

A Brazilian army officer, Edmundo de Barros, conceived the idea of creating a nature reserve around the waterfalls in 1897. Two separate parks were established by the Argentine and Brazilian governments. The Argentine national park covers 132,500 acres (53,623 ha) of tropical jungle. A wildlife reserve shelters hundreds of species of birds, reptiles, and fish, and many species of butterflies, orchids, monkeys, parrots, and pumas. The national park is a nature lover's paradise because of the myriad species of tropical flora found there.

UNESCO declared the Iguazú Falls a World Heritage Site in 1986.

wheat, corn, flax, and alfalfa—are grown in the rich soil of the Pampas. Although there is plenty of rain in the eastern Pampas—about 40 inches (102 centimeters) a year—the climate is drier on the western plains, where vast herds of cattle graze.

THE ANDES

The western part of Argentina, bordering Chile, is marked by the huge Andes mountain range. Although the earliest Spanish settlements were located in the Andes, only about 15 percent of the population currently lives in this rugged area. A small group of indigenous Indians raise sheep in the northern part of the Argentine Andes. Miners dig for iron ore, uranium, and other metals in this region.

Just east of the Andes lies a region called the Piedmont. Farmers grow crops for export such as sugarcane, corn, cotton, and fruit in the low mountains and desert valleys in this region. Most Argentine wines are made from the grapes of San Juan in the vineyards near Mendoza in the Piedmont. The region's dry climate, sandy soil, and year-round sunshine are ideal for the wine industry.

West of Mendoza rises Mount Aconcagua, the highest peak in the Western Hemisphere. *Aconcagua* means "stone guard" in an indigenous dialect. The Uspallata Pass, located near Mount Aconcagua, leads into Chile at a height of 12,500 feet (3,810 m).

PATAGONIA

Patagonia covers more than a quarter of Argentina. The region has dry, windswept plateaus, deep canyons, and stretches of cool desert under the shadow of the Andes. Western Patagonia boasts beautiful resort areas around lakes and mountains; the far south has a cool, foggy, and stormy climate. Patagonia does not experience summer, but ocean currents help moderate winter temperatures. Only about 1—3 percent of Argentina's population lives in Patagonia.

At the southern tip of South America is the island of Tierra del Fuego or "Land of Fire." In 1520 Ferdinand de Magellan named the island after the Ona and Yagana Indian campfires he saw there. In the 1880s European settlers and Chileans arrived on the island. They built large ranches for raising sheep and irrigated farmlands to grow vegetables and fruit. One-third of Tierra del Fuego is Argentine territory; the rest of the islands belong to Chile.

The southernmost town in the world, Ushuaia, is situated in Argentina. Ushuaia's weather is almost always chilly, and the nearby mountains are usually snowcapped. Approximately 60,813 people who live in Ushuaia can look south, across the waters of the Beagle Channel, toward the South Pole, some 650 miles (1,046 km) away. People in Ushuaia have only about seven hours of daylight in the winter. In the summer they enjoy daylight for about 17 hours each day.

ARGENTINA'S WATERS

More than 1,600 miles (2,574 km) of Argentina's length is bounded by the Atlantic Ocean and is dotted with large bays. The longest river in Argentina is the Paraná River, second in South America after the Amazon River. The Río de la Plata is the river and estuary formed by the confluence of the Uruguay River and the Paraná River on the border between Argentina and Uruguay. The Paraná River and its tributaries drain northern and much of central Argentina. The Río de la Plata and the Paraná River are natural boundaries and important arteries in Argentina.

The drainage patterns of Argentina's rivers and lakes are greatly affected by the height of the Andes Mountains. In the south a number of Argentine lakes empty into the Pacific Ocean through Chile. After heavy rains, however, these lakes pour their extra water into the Atlantic Ocean.

The Perito Moreno Glacier is the world's third-largest reserve of fresh water.

THE WORLD'S OLDEST DINOSAUR

In 1988 a scientist from the University of Chicago made an amazing discovery. He and his team uncovered the full skeleton of the oldest dinosaur ever recorded. The discoverers named the dinosaur Herrerasaurus to honor Victorino Herrera, the goat farmer who led them to the find. It is estimated that Herrerasaurus lived 230 million years ago, when most of the Earth's land formed a single supercontinent called Pangaea. The meat-eating Herrerasaurus was about 6 feet (1.8 m) long and weighed 300 pounds (136 kg). It had sharp teeth like a shark's, talons like an eagle's, and hind legs like those of an ostrich.

"The Argentine lake region . . . is cold, the vegetation ancient; silent and solitary forests end at silent lakes that mirror snowy hills resplendent in the sun." —Jorge Luis Borges

Visitors to Argentina are often impressed by the country's unique natural beauty. Lake Nahuel Huapí covers 204 square miles (529 square km) at 2,510 feet (770 m) above sea level. This beautiful lake is located in a nature reserve and resort area in the southern Andes. The Perito Moreno Glacier in Patagonia moves 5 yards (4.5 m) a day, shattering icebergs in its path and raising a dramatic explosion of spray.

COLORFUL WILDLIFE

A variety of animals lives in Argentina, including the armadillo, opossum, coatimundi, tapir, jaguar, howler monkey, giant anteater, and puma (or mountain lion).

The Perito Moreno Glacier located in Los Glaciares National Park is one of the 48 glaciers in the region.

Some unusual species are also found. The guanaco is a small animal related to the camel but with no hump. It is the common ancestor of the llama, alpaca, and vicuña, animals that roam the northern Andean plateau. The vizcacha burrows underground tunnels in the Pampas. These tunnels often trip horses and cattle. The capybara of the tropical forests is the world's largest rodent. It can weigh more than 110 pounds (50 kilograms). The Patagonian cavy is similar to the guinea pig.

Visitors to Patagonia are impressed by the picturesque wildlife of the southern coasts. A large number of dolphins, penguins, and sea lions make their home in this region. The Valdés Peninsula, a large nature reserve on the Atlantic coast, supports herds of huge elephant seals; guanacos, camel-like animals; and groups of large ostrich-like birds called rheas, among many other species of birds and animals.

Argentine birds include flamingos, herons, parrots, black-necked swans, and crested screamers. Other birds, such as the tinamou, a relative of the ostrich; the albatross, a large, web-footed seabird; and the Andean condor, a vulture currently in danger of extinction, also live in Argentina.

Lake Nahuel Huapí's crystal-clear waters are very susceptible to climate changes and have an average surface temperature of 45°F (7°C). This makes it both beautiful and treacherous. Hypothermia is one of the risks bathers must face.

INTERNET LINKS

www.argentina.gov.ar

This site provides information about the geography and climate of Argentina.

www.argentina.org.au/geography.htm

This site provides information about the geography and climate of Argentina, including very useful information on the various regions of Argentina.

http://geography.howstuffworks.com/south-america/geography-of-argentina1.htm

This site includes concise facts about the geography of Argentina.

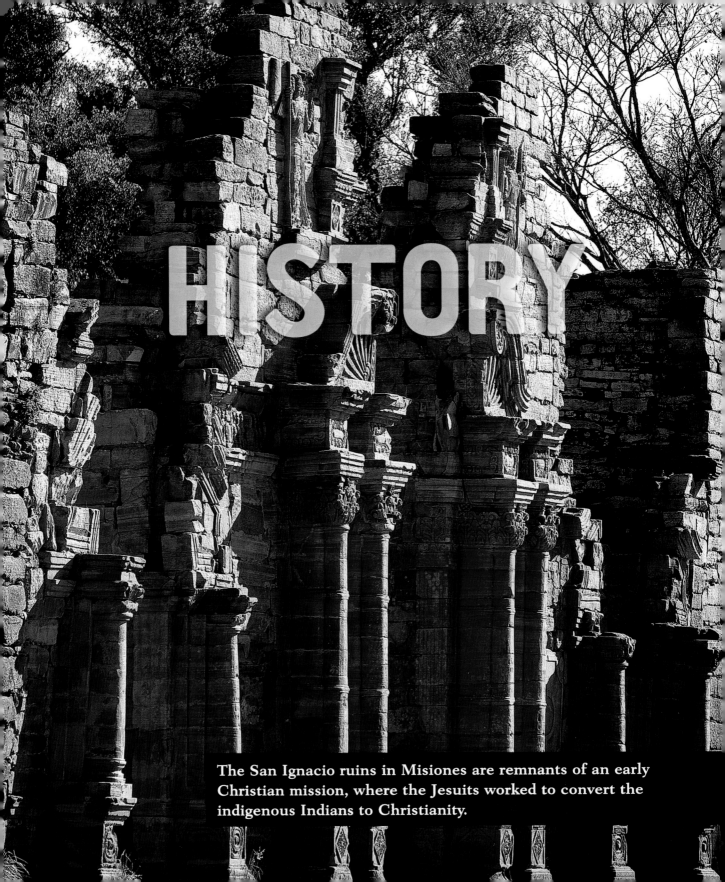

HISTORY

The San Ignacio ruins in Misiones are remnants of an early Christian mission, where the Jesuits worked to convert the indigenous Indians to Christianity.

2

ARGENTINA'S INDIGENOUS PEOPLES hunted and gathered across the Chaco, the Pampas, and Patagonia. They originated in Asia and crossed the Bering Strait that joined Siberia with North America in prehistoric times.

EARLY PEOPLE

When the first European settlers arrived, approximately 300,000 indigenous Indians lived in Argentina. A combination of war, diseases brought by the Europeans such as smallpox and measles, and intermarriage greatly reduced the indigenous population. Today between 3 and 5 percent of Argentines are pure Indians. In some provinces the indigenous population accounts for between 17 and 25 percent of the population.

EXPLORERS ARRIVE

The first European to land in Argentina was reportedly Juan Díaz de Solís, a Portuguese explorer who sailed into the Río de la Plata estuary in 1516. Solís claimed the land for Spain but was killed by indigenous Indians during a later landing venture. In 1520 Portuguese explorer Ferdinand de Magellan stopped at the same river on his historic voyage around the world.

In 1527 Sebastian Cabot, an Italian serving the Spanish Crown, founded the first European settlement near present-day Rosario. It was Cabot who named the river Río de la Plata, or River of Silver, after the silver jewelry worn by the local Indians.

Historians divide the history of Argentina into four main sections: the pre-Columbian time or early history (up to the 16th century), the colonial period (roughly 1516–1810), the independence wars and the early postcolonial period of the nation (1810–80), and the history of modern Argentina from around 1880.

THE COLONIAL PERIOD The history of Argentina is part of the larger story of the conquest and colonization of South America by the Spanish and the Portuguese. The conquest of the Inca Empire of Peru in 1532 by Francisco Pizarro opened the way for the colonists. Most of the Spaniards who arrived by sea were eventually driven away by the indigenous Indians and the fear of starvation. The Spaniards who finally settled in Argentina came mainly from Peru and Chile by crossing over the Andes. They founded Argentina's oldest cities—Jujuy, Salta, Tucumán, Mendoza, and Córdoba—in the late 1500s. Argentina was part of the Viceroyalty of Peru until 1776, when the Viceroyalty of the Río de la Plata was established. Horses, sheep, and cattle brought from Spain easily multiplied in the fertile new land.

During the 1600s Spain's economy declined. The Spanish government was forced to sell large plots of land in Argentina. Rich Europeans and criollos, or people of Spanish descent born in Latin America, bought the land and established huge estates. To herd their wild cattle the owners hired gauchos, who were usually mestizos, or people of mixed indigenous Indian and Spanish blood.

The Cabildo in Buenos Aires used to house the Spanish colonial government.

INDEPENDENCE

In time wealthy landowners began to resent the Spanish government's interference in their business affairs. The landowners wanted to control trade and keep the wealth they produced at home rather than send it to Spain in the form of taxes to the Spanish Crown.

Later, when France attacked Spain in 1807—08, Argentina's criollos took advantage of Spain's military vulnerability to fight for their independence. Eventually, on May 25, 1810, Argentina declared its independence, but King Ferdinand of Spain refused to acknowledge this declaration.

The Argentine national hero, General José de San Martín (1778—1850), urged Argentine leaders to formally declare independence from Spain. They did so in Tucumán on July 9, 1816, and the leaders named their country the United Provinces of the River Plate.

San Martín then led an expedition across the Andes into Chile and helped drive out Spanish troops there and in Peru, ending Spanish domination in South America.

José de San Martín is also known as El Libertador, or "the liberator," for his leadership in the fight for independence from Spain in South America. Monuments dedicated to El Libertador dominate the main squares of cities, towns, and villages throughout the country.

FORGING A NATION

The next 50 years were marked by two major issues: the struggle for power between Buenos Aires and the provinces and political turmoil under unstable governments. The *porteños* (por-TAY-nyos), or residents of the port city of Buenos Aires, quarreled with the ranchers in the provinces over control of the country's rural areas. These conflicts almost destroyed trade and the entire Argentine economy.

A constitution drawn up in 1826 gave Buenos Aires control over the interior. The first president of Argentina, Bernardino Rivadavia, was a *porteño*. However, he was soon overthrown by the rival political party of the rural ranchers, whose leader was later killed by members of Rivadavia's party.

Dictator Juan Manuel de Rosas (1793–1877) was an Argentine soldier, gaucho cowboy, and dictator who ruled Argentina for over 20 years, from 1829 to 1852.

The next ruler was a type that would appear frequently in Argentine history—the strongman or caudillo. Juan Manuel de Rosas (1793—1877), a landowner from the Pampas, ruled Argentina from 1829 to 1852. He persecuted and murdered many of his political enemies and wiped out a large number of indigenous Indians. Rosas was finally overthrown by General Justo José de Urquiza. Rosas escaped to England, where he spent the rest of his life in exile.

THE CONSTITUTION OF 1853

A new constitution, proclaimed in 1853, was based on the model of the U.S. Constitution. Urquiza became president of a new confederation of provinces. In 1860 Argentina officially adopted its present name and the province of Buenos Aires at first refused to join the confederation, becoming a member only after a civil war. Buenos Aires then became the nation's capital. General Bartolomé Mitre took over as president of the 14 united provinces of the Argentine Republic.

During this period President Domingo Faustino Sarmiento (1811—88), who ruled Argentina from 1868 to 1874, vigorously promoted public education. Today the country has one of the highest literacy rates in the world—97.2 percent.

Pressure to obtain more grazing land resulted in the Indian Wars of the late 1870s and early 1880s. During these battles indigenous Indians in the Pampas and in Patagonia were virtually exterminated. Their lands were taken by officers who had led the war against them.

In 1880 the city of Buenos Aires became a federal district, similar to the District of Columbia in the United States.

THE GOLDEN AGE

Some historians call the years from 1880 to the outbreak of World War I in 1914 "the Golden Age" of Argentina's history. Huge numbers of immigrants and a great deal of foreign investment arrived in the country from Europe. A land of natural resources and frontier wilderness, Argentina seemed destined to become one of the world's richest and most powerful nations by the early 20th century. The railroad system expanded rapidly. Refrigerated ships began to carry beef and hides to Europe in 1877, and exports of farm products grew rapidly. Sheep farming became more prominent. By the 1880s wool constituted at least half of Argentina's exports.

This illustration from the early 1800s shows European immigrants disembarking at the bay of Buenos Aires.

During this period streets were paved, broad avenues and parks were built, and majestic public buildings and private homes sprang up. Argentina became the most urbanized country in Latin America.

Starting in 1929, the Great Depression, triggered by the U.S. stock market crash, had an enormous effect on Argentina's economy. Heavily dependent on the export market, the Argentine economy declined sharply during this time. The government of President Hipólito Irigoyen was not able to solve the economic crisis. Army leaders seized this opportunity to remove the president from office in 1930 and install a military government, followed by a series of military dictatorships.

THE PERÓN ERA

The most famous strongman leader in Argentina's history, Colonel Juan Domingo Perón (1895—1974), rose to power during the military regimes of the 1930s and 1940s. He served as Minister of Labor in a junta (a group of military leaders) and became president in 1946. He appealed to the working classes by giving the people higher wages, pensions, and other benefits, and by strengthening their unions. His supporters formed the Perónist party, which remains influential to this day.

After being suppressed for many years by military dictatorships, Perón's party returned to power with the support of the people in 1973.

Before Perón, foreign countries had tremendous power over Argentina's economy. The British controlled most of the railroads. The United States controlled the automotive business. Even the meat-packing industry was dominated by foreigners. Perón increased government spending, took control of many of the country's industries, and built up manufacturing at the expense of farm production, which he taxed heavily. The resulting drop in farm production caused the national income to fall.

Perón ignored civil liberties. He suspended freedom of the press and freedom of speech, altered the constitution to increase his powers, and permitted himself a second term of office, even though it was not allowed under the 1853 constitution. He remained popular with some Argentines because of his personal charm and his appeal to the working masses. During his second term, however, his power and popularity declined. He lost the support of the Catholic Church and alienated the army and the navy. Perón fled Argentina in 1955 and eventually settled in Spain. He left a legacy of debt and inflation, yet his ideas continue to appeal to many Argentines.

DISRUPTION

Military dictators alternated with civilian presidents during the years of Perón's exile. In 1956 Perón's constitution of 1949 was replaced by the original constitution of 1853. Taking an anti-Perónist stance, the military government dissolved Perón's political party. The most noted president of this period, Arturo Frondizi (1958—62), won the presidency with the support of the Perónist factions of rival political parties. He promised to re-establish the Perónist party in exchange for their support.

EVITA PERÓN

Perón's beautiful second wife, Eva Duarte de Perón, a former actress, was a powerful leader in her own right until her early death at the age of 33 from cancer. Known as Evita, she was idolized by the urban working class. Evita gained the right to vote for women in 1947 and founded women's political and social service organizations. Her work brought health and welfare benefits to the poor. The masses expressed their affection for Evita by staging huge rallies where she delivered powerful and dramatic speeches. For many, her magnificent jewels and gowns and her rags-to-riches story symbolized a proud and wealthy Argentina.

Evita was born in the poor village of Los Toldos in 1919. She went to Buenos Aires in her teens and became a popular radio actress. Perón, a widower, was 48 and Evita was 24 when they met. She greatly assisted his rise to power. Perón's popularity dropped significantly after her death. Many Argentines viewed Evita as a saint, but the Catholic Church in Rome resisted all pressure to canonize her. Her epitaph in La Recoleta cemetery reads, "Don't cry for me, Argentina, I remain quite near to you."

After a period of strikes and political unrest, the military allowed a Perónist named Héctor José Cámpora to become president in 1973. Later that year Perón returned from exile. Cámpora resigned, enabling Perón to be elected president in October 1973. Perón named his third wife, Isabel, vice president and governed briefly until his death the following year at the age of 79.

After Perón's death Isabel became the first woman president in the history of Argentina. During her presidency inflation rose to over 400 percent and terrorist acts, mainly by a left-wing guerrilla group called the Montoneros, plagued the country.

THE "DIRTY WAR"

In 1976 military leaders then arrested Isabel Perón. They seized the government, dissolved the congress, outlawed all political parties, censored the press, and banned all strikes. The National Reorganization Process was the name used by its leaders for the military government that ruled Argentina from 1976 to 1983. The expression was used to imply orderliness and control of the critical sociopolitical situation of Argentina at the time.

Mothers carry photographs of their lost loved ones as they peacefully demonstrate around the Plaza de Mayo each Thursday. According to a report published in 1986, almost 9,000 Argentines disappeared during the "dirty war."

The new leaders began what is known as the *guerra sucia* (GAY-rah SUE-see-ah), or "dirty war," against the terrorists. The military government was able to destroy the power of guerrilla groups, but in their campaign, they condoned violence against thousands of innocent people. The government kidnapped and killed many of its opponents, without revealing their fates. These political victims became known as *los desaparecidos* (lohs day-sah-pah-ray-SEE-dohs) or "the disappeared."

Mothers of the disappeared began to demonstrate every Thursday in the Plaza de Mayo, outside the government palace. These women were later called the "Mothers of the Plaza de Mayo." Later investigations revealed that most of the disappeared had been killed. Hundreds of detention centers had been used to torture and kill people. Mass graves were discovered. A government commission described this period as the "greatest tragedy of our history, and the most savage."

THE FALKLANDS WAR AND DEMOCRACY

Argentina's economy worsened during the Falklands War in 1982. At this time the public image of the regime was eroded by corruption, a failing economy, and growing public awareness of the harsh repressive measures taken by the regime. Although Great Britain had occupied the islands since 1833, Argentina had claimed sovereignty over them since the early 1800s. The Islas Malvinas, as the islands are called in Argentina, lie about 300 miles (483 km) off the coast of Argentina. The residents are British subjects.

President Leopoldo Galtieri, an army general, hoped to unite the Argentine people behind his government by occupying the islands and taking them back from the British. Argentine troops fought in the air, at sea, and on the islands, but failed to repel the British army. The war lasted 72 tragic days, taking 2,000 Argentine and British lives.

When Argentina surrendered, it did not give up its claim to the islands. Great Britain maintains a 2,500-man garrison in the Falklands.

It was not until seven years after the war that Argentina and Great Britain resumed consular ties, air and sea links, and unrestricted trade.

The military defeat in the war led to a call for free elections. Raúl Alfonsín became president in December 1983, restoring the constitution of 1853. Alfonsín brought to trial the military commanders responsible for the "dirty war." Nine commanders were tried, and five received prison sentences. The military was able to prevent the prosecution of lower-ranking officers who claimed they were only following orders.

Economic woes—inflation, unemployment, and falling wages—damaged Alfonsín's popularity. In May 1989 Perónist Carlos Menem was elected president. Riots over high food prices led Alfonsín to resign in June, allowing Menem to take office five months early. Menem altered the constitution in 1994 to allow himself to run for a second term, which he won. In 1999 Fernando de la Rúa won the election.

President de la Rúa had extensive political experience. He was elected chief of government of Buenos Aires in 1996. Toward the end of 2001, Argentina faced grave economic problems. The International Monetary Fund (IMF) pressed Argentina to start paying its external debt. Voters reacted to

The Falkland Islands Defense Force (FIDF) is the locally maintained volunteer defense unit in the Falkland Islands. The FIDF works alongside the military units supplied by the United Kingdom to ensure the security of the islands.

the rapidly worsening economy in the October 2001 midterm elections by depriving de la Rúa's party of its majority in the Lower House and also by casting a record 25 percent of spoiled ballots. Spoiled ballots are voting slips regarded by the election authorities to be invalid and thus not included in the final tally.

The overall economy declined drastically during December 2001. The resulting riots led to dozens of deaths. On December 20 de la Rúa resigned. Finally, on January 2, 2002, the National Congress elected the Perónist Eduardo Duhalde, a losing candidate in the most recent presidential election, as president. The peso was first devalued (lost its value) by 29 percent, and then the pegging of the Argentine peso to the U.S. dollar was abandoned; by July 2002 the national currency had depreciated to one-quarter of its former value.

President Duhalde faced a country in turmoil. His administration had to deal with a wave of protests with a relatively tolerant policy, intending to minimize violence. As inflation (rise in prices of goods and services) became a serious issue and the effects of the crisis became apparent in the form of increased unemployment and poverty, Duhalde chose a moderate, low-

A memorial in Ushuaia remembers the 368 crew members aboard the ship *General Belgrano* who were lost in the war between Argentina and England over the Falkland Islands.

profile economist, Roberto Lavagna, as his Minister of Economy. In general, the economic measures implemented brought inflation under control.

After a year Duhalde deemed his tasks fulfilled and, pressured by certain political factors, he called for elections, which brought Néstor Kirchner, the left-of-center Perónist governor of Santa Cruz, to power in April 2003.

President Kirchner took office on May 25, 2003. He reshuffled the leadership of the armed forces, overturned controversial amnesty laws that protected members of the 1976—83 dictatorship from prosecution, and kept Lavagna on as economy minister for most of his presidency. Kirchner's administration saw a strong economic rebound and foreign debt restructuring.

The 2007 general election took place in 10 provinces in September and Kirchner's Front for Victory won in six provinces. On December 10, 2007, Cristina Fernández de Kirchner took over the presidency from her husband, after winning the elections with 44 percent of the vote. She kept many of her husband's ministers. However, in contrast with her husband's administration, which was seen as somewhat isolationist, Fernández has shown interest in promoting better ties with other countries.

In March 2010 Fernández made a historic amends trip to Peru, a country with which relations had been adversely affected following the Carlos Menem administration's illegal sale of weapons to Ecuador in the 1990s.

INTERNET LINKS

http://topics.nytimes.com/top/reference/timestopics/people/k/cristina_fernandez_de_kirchner/index.html

This site has an archive of articles from *The New York Times* about Cristina Kirchner and her presidency.

www.state.gov/r/pa/ei/bgn/26516.htm#history

This site provides a concise overview of the history of Argentina.

www.evitaperon.org/

This site provides information about the life of Evita Perón as well as the work she accomplished through the Eva Perón Foundation.

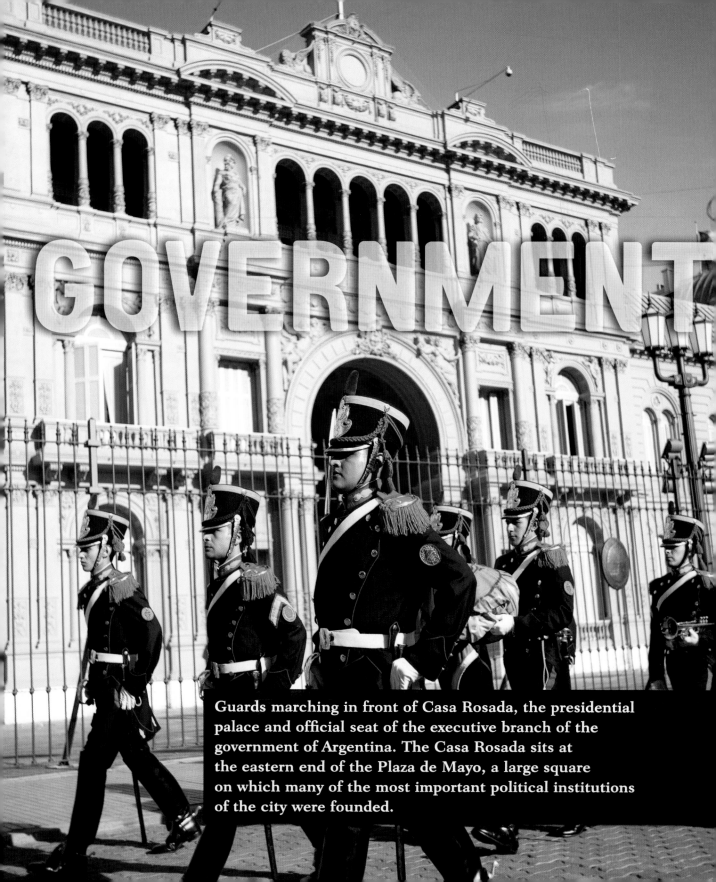

GOVERNMENT

Guards marching in front of Casa Rosada, the presidential palace and official seat of the executive branch of the government of Argentina. The Casa Rosada sits at the eastern end of the Plaza de Mayo, a large square on which many of the most important political institutions of the city were founded.

3

ARGENTINA'S OFFICIAL NAME IS *República Argentina*, or Argentine Republic. The republic was established on May 1, 1853, the year the constitution was adopted. Like the U.S. constitution, the Argentine constitution calls for an elected president and Congress. The president and vice president must be born in Argentina. They serve a four-year term and can be re-elected once. Every Argentine who is 18 years and older can vote.

The government of Argentina, functioning within the framework of a federal system, is a presidential representative democratic republic.

The Congress building in Buenos Aires was completed in 1906.

The Palace of Justice (supreme court) is a Greek revival building in Libertad Square, Buenos Aires.

Power is divided among the executive, legislative, and judicial branches of the government. This creates a system of checks and balances, which is meant to prevent one person or branch from gaining complete control of the nation.

The president appoints a cabinet of ministers to head the executive departments of the government. The vice president leads the senate and becomes president if the president can no longer serve.

The Argentine Congress is made up of two houses: the Chamber of Deputies and the Senate. The Chamber of Deputies has 257 members who are elected directly by the people. The deputies serve for 4 years. The Senate consists of 72 members chosen by the provincial legislatures. Three senators represent each of the 23 provinces and the Federal District of Buenos Aires. Senators serve for 6 years.

In 2001 a new electoral system for the senate took effect. Since then, every 2 years, each one of the 24 electoral districts (the 23 provinces and the autonomous city of Buenos Aires) has elected one-half of their senate representatives.

THE JUDICIARY

The last execution in Argentina took place in 1916.

The Argentine judiciary, or system of courts and judges, is influenced by the judicial systems of the United States and Western Europe. With approval from the senate, the president appoints the nine members of the Supreme Court and the judges of the Federal Courts of Appeal. All judges are appointed for life.

Each province has its own system of lower and higher courts. Judges in the provinces are appointed by the local governors. Local governments have limited powers because the president can remove the governor of a province and call for new provincial elections.

The constitution establishes trial by jury for criminal cases, but this is rarely practiced. The death penalty was reintroduced in 1976—more as a deterrent than as punishment—for the killing of government, military police, and judicial officials and for other terrorist activities. But by 2008 the death penalty had been legally abolished.

THE ARMED FORCES

The president is commander in chief of the armed forces. Military conscription, a system that requires young, healthy male—and at times female—citizens to serve in the nation's armed forces for a specific number of years, was abolished in 1995.

At times the armed forces have been Argentina's strongest political force. Argentine military leaders have overthrown civilian governments on many occasions during the last century. Some of these military coups were bloody, whereas others were less violent.

The constitution of 1853 guaranteed Argentines freedom of speech and religion and gave them the right of public assembly and private property. These and other supposedly inalienable civil liberties often suffered under military regimes. In addition the "dirty war" was the only time in the history of the republic when the government actually set aside and ignored the constitution to achieve its goals.

Because military takeovers have often disrupted constitutional governments in Argentina, no Argentine president in the last century has been able to achieve the government's goals or remain in office long without the support of the military. The greatest challenge in governing Argentina has been to develop a democratic government stable enough to withstand the pressure and demands of powerful self-interest groups and the military.

The acrimony between Cristina Kirchner's government and the national media was exacerbated by a series of lock-ins carried out by the truck drivers' union, led by Pablo Moyano, son of Hugo Moyano, a close ally of the Kirchner government. During the lock-in, the country's most widely circulated newspapers (*Clarín* and *La Nación*) were prevented from distributing papers to newsstands by force and threats of violence.

THE STATE FLAG AND THE COAT OF ARMS

A sun with a human face, called the "Sun of May," appears on the national flag, which was adopted in 1818, and on the coat of arms. The sun represents Argentina's freedom from Spain. The colors, light blue and white, were worn by Argentine soldiers who fought off British invaders in 1806—07.

The coat of arms shows two hands clasped and surrounded by a laurel wreath. The background colors match the colors of the flag. In the back is a red "liberty cap" on a pole. The sun rises from the top of the wreath.

CRISTINA FERNÁNDEZ DE KIRCHNER

Cristina Elisabet Fernández de Kirchner, commonly known as Cristina Fernández or Cristina Kirchner, is the current president of Argentina and the widow of former president Néstor Kirchner. She is Argentina's first elected female president.

Fernández is a graduate of the National University of La Plata. She met her husband during her studies, and they moved to Santa Cruz to work as lawyers. In May 1991 she was elected to the provincial legislature. Between 1995 and 2007 she was repeatedly elected to the Argentine National Congress, both as a national deputy and as a national senator. During Kirchner's presidency (2003—07) she acted as First Lady. Fernández was chosen as the Front for Victory presidential candidate in 2007, and in the October 2007 general election she obtained 45.3 percent of the vote. The transition from Néstor Kirchner (her husband and the previous president) to Cristina Kirchner was also the first time when a democratic head of state was replaced by his spouse, without involving the death of either. Néstor Kirchner stayed active in politics despite not being the president and worked alongside Cristina Kirchner. The press developed the term *presidential marriage* to refer both of them at once.

Fernández's term has not been without controversy. She faces the challenges of inflation, union demands for higher salaries, and lack of

Some political analysts compared this type of government with a diarchy. A diarchy is a form of government in which two individuals, the diarchs, are the heads of state.

institutional credibility. Her plan to raise levies on soybean exports from 35 to 44 percent was torpedoed by her own vice president, and she has a tumultuous relationship with the media.

Her government contends that the Clarín Group (which controls television, radio, newspapers, cable services, Internet companies, and until recently, the monopoly for soccer in Argentina) has a policy of monopolization, whereas the Clarín media conglomerate considers that the acts of the government run contrary to freedom of speech. Not surprisingly there have been many negative articles about her government in the Clarín newspapers. However, she has managed to break the Clarín Group's monopoly on the media by allowing other players into the media market.

In 2010 Kirchner was ranked third by *TIME* magazine on a list of the top 10 female leaders in the world. In 2010 *FORBES* ranked her 68th out of the most powerful 100 women in the world.

Cristina Kirchner, the 55th and current president of Argentina, is the country's first elected female president and the widow of former president Néstor Kirchner.

INTERNET LINKS

https://www.cia.gov/library/publications/the-world-factbook/geos/ ar.html

This website provides current government initiatives and other relevant topics.

www.atfa.org/

This site contains news about the negotiations between the Argentine and the American governments, especially about Argentina's debt.

http://news.bbc.co.uk/2/hi/americas/country_profiles/1192478.stm

This site provides a lot of fascinating news articles about Argentina.

ECONOMY

Avenida Nueve de Julio in Buenos Aires is the heartbeat of the city with its skyscapers and endless roads.

4

THE SPANISH EXPLORERS NAMED Argentina after the silver they expected to find in the new land. In the end they did not find mineral resources. So instead they brought cattle and sheep from Europe and cultivated wheat and other grains. These became Argentina's main economic resources. The country is also one of the Group of 20 major economies. The Group of 20 consists of 19 countries, of which Argentina is one, and the European Union.

Argentina benefits from its rich natural resources, a highly literate population, an export-oriented agricultural sector, and a diversified industrial base.

A salt extraction pool in Salinas Grandes, Jujuy.

Food in Argentina is plentiful and relatively cheap. The poverty, starvation, and malnutrition that plague many countries on the South American continent were virtually unknown in Argentina until the numerous economic crises that it overcame after 2002.

Half of Argentina's total land area is used for pasture. In the roughly 10 percent of the land that is cultivated for crops, the soil is rich and productive. The main farm crops include corn, wheat, soybeans, and sorghum. Grapes, apples, citrus fruits, sugarcane, yerba mate, tobacco, cotton, and tea are also grown. From grapes come a variety of fine wines.

A sheep herd in the Falkland Islands. Early explorers expected to find huge deposits of silver in Argentina. Instead they found wealth in the rich soil and vast grazing lands.

Many people are employed in agriculture, which accounts for 7.5 percent of Argentina's gross domestic product (GDP) and one-fifth of all exports.

Argentina is famous for beef production. The British cattle breeds of Aberdeen Angus, Hereford, and Shorthorn, and the French Charolais are particularly popular. Patagonia and other dry parts of Argentina are sheep-breeding regions; sheep's wool is a major export.

Farmers raise large numbers of pigs and poultry. The dairy industry is also quite extensive.

Argentine agriculture is relatively capital intensive, providing about 7 percent of all employment today. It accounts for less than 10 percent of the Argentine GDP.

MANUFACTURING AND SERVICE INDUSTRIES

The manufacturing sector accounts for about 21.2 percent of Argentina's GDP and employs close to one-fifth of the workforce. Argentina's industrial base is quite diverse, thanks to the bounty of the Pampas. The chief industry remains the processing of meat and other food products. Other industries include textiles, leather goods, chemicals, metals, printing, lumber, fishing, automobiles, railroad cars, and consumer goods. The factories are highly concentrated in and around Buenos Aires.

The service sector accounts for 59.8 percent of Argentina's GDP and employs 72 percent of the workforce. Workers in the service sector include those in the local, state, and federal governments; the military; schools; hospitals; stores; restaurants; and banks. Also of particular importance are workers in the fields of transportation and communications, because their contributions help build the infrastructure of the economy.

An oil refinery in the extreme southeast of the country. Oil derricks are a common sight in Argentina. The country is self-sufficient in crude petroleum and petroleum products.

NATURAL RESOURCES

In addition to the rich, fertile soil of the Pampas, Argentina has abundant natural resources. It has enough natural gas reserves to last at least another 60 years. An extensive pipeline system links the natural gas fields with important industrial centers.

Oil and hydroelectric energy sources are being developed. Petroleum supplies about 70 percent of the energy used in Argentina. The most important oil fields are located in Patagonia and the Piedmont. Argentina is one of the chief oil-producing countries in Latin America. Around 46 million cubic yards (35 million cubic meters) of petroleum and petroleum fuels are produced a year, as well as 65 billion cubic yards (50 billion cubic meters) of natural gas, making the nation self-sufficient in these staples, and generating around 10 percent of exports. The Yacyreta hydroelectric dam, with 3,500 megawatts of installed capacity, is the largest power plant in Argentina. Argentina and co-owner Paraguay share the electricity generated from Yacyreta evenly, with almost all of Paraguay's share being exported to Argentina. The 1,890-megawatt Salto Grande is another binational project, owned by the governments of Argentina and Uruguay. It is estimated that Argentina has used only 20 percent of its hydroelectric potential.

Argentina is one of six countries that supply 90 percent of the world's grain supply. The other countries are Thailand, Australia, Canada, France, and the United States.

Loggers transporting tree trunks in Argentina. Argentina is famous for the Quebracho tree. The tree yields hard wood that can be used as building material, and its extract is used for tanning hides.

Argentina's mineral reserves are still largely untouched. Among the minerals found in the country are beryllium, coal, copper, iron, lead, manganese, tin, tungsten, and zinc.

Although there are large forest reserves, especially in the northeast and the south, the timber industry is still fairly small. Of the 26 million cubic yards (20 million cubic meters) of wood stock available in Argentina, only 10 million (7.6 million cubic meters) are harvested for timber. Ninety-five percent of Argentina's timber comes from planted forests, and 1.2 million out of an available 2.7 of 12.4 million acres (5 million ha) are planted. The forestry industry employs half a million Argentineans.

The government and private companies are investing in the development of the nation's resources. This has led to the exploitation of new quarries, mines, and oil wells. The building of new roads, dams, and factories has also created new job opportunities and fostered development in rural areas and economic growth.

Argentina is an important regional producer of minerals, including primary aluminum, lead, copper, zinc, silver, and gold.

IMPORTS AND EXPORTS

Argentina exports about two-thirds more than it imports. Its chief exports are soybeans, petroleum and gas, vehicles, corn, and wheat. Exports to Brazil account for 19 percent of Argentina's total export figures; its exports to China account for 9 percent; its exports to Chile account for 7 percent; and its exports to the United States account for 6 percent of its total export figures.

Argentina's chief imports include industrial chemicals, nonelectrical machinery, transportation equipment, iron, steel, and coffee. Its imports from the European Union account for 28 percent of Argentina's total imports, the United States accounts for 22 percent, and Brazil accounts for 21 percent.

To further improve the balance of trade, Argentina strives to increase the production of goods for the export market by manufacturing products locally. It now produces nearly all the consumer goods it once imported, such as cars, refrigerators, and television sets. One drawback of this policy is the fact that Argentines may miss out on buying cheaper goods made in countries with low labor costs.

The container harbor in Buenos Aires. Argentina is one of the world's biggest producers and exporters of beef, wool, wine, and wheat.

INFLATION AND FOREIGN DEBT

The people of Argentina enjoy one of the highest standards of living in South America, yet the modern Argentine economy pales in comparison with past statistics. In the 1920s Argentina was the eighth-largest economy in the world; by 1987 its economy ranked 58th worldwide.

In the 1930s, after World War I and the Great Depression, the Argentine government began an economic strategy known as import substitution. By imposing high tariffs on all imported goods, the government aimed to protect, and thereby develop, local industries. The goal of the governments at the time and during the following 40 years was to make Argentina a self-sufficient country, producing its own agricultural and manufactured goods, especially during the Perón era. By the 1970s this goal had been achieved. The government's focus on industrial development, however, resulted in poorer agricultural output. In addition high government spending on the industrial sector as well as heavy borrowing from international funds caused exorbitant inflation rates in the 1980s, rising as high as 1,000 percent.

THE ARGENTINE ECONOMIC CRISIS

In 1983 inflation in Argentina started to spiral out of control. In 1989 Argentina's inflation topped 5,000 percent for the year. In 1991 Domingo Cavallo restored the peso as the Argentine currency with the value fixed to the U.S. dollar. As a result of the convertibility law inflation dropped sharply, price stability was ensured, and the value of the currency was preserved. However, Argentina still had external debts to pay and it needed to keep borrowing money. The fixed exchange rate made imports cheap, producing a constant flight of dollars away from the country, and a progressive loss of Argentina's industrial infrastructure, which led to an increase in unemployment.

By 1999 newly elected president Fernando de la Rúa faced a country where unemployment had risen to a critical point and the undesirable effects of the fixed exchange rate were showing forcefully. In 1999 Argentina's GDP dropped 4 percent, and the country entered a recession that lasted three years, ending in a collapse.

Argentina quickly lost the confidence of investors, and the flight of money away from the country increased. In 2001 people fearing the worst began to withdraw large sums of money from their bank accounts, turning pesos into dollars and sending them abroad, causing a run on the banks. The government then enacted a set of measures (informally known as the corralito *[kor-rah-LIT-toh]) that effectively froze all bank accounts for 12 months, allowing for only minor sums of cash to be withdrawn.*

Because of this allowance limit and the serious problems it caused in certain cases, many Argentines became enraged and took to the streets of important cities, especially Buenos Aires. They engaged in a form of popular protest that became known as cacerolazo *(banging pots and pans). At first the* cacerolazos *were simply noisy demonstrations, but soon they included property destruction. Confrontations between the police and the citizens became a common sight, and fires were also set on Buenos Aires avenues. Fernando de la Rúa declared a state of emergency, but this only worsened the situation, precipitating the violent protests of December 20 and 21, 2001, in Plaza de Mayo, where demonstrators clashed with the police, ended with several dead, and precipitated the fall of the government. De la Rúa eventually fled the Casa Rosada in a helicopter on December 21.*

During the last week of 2001 the interim government led by Rodríguez Saá, facing the impossibility of meeting debt payments. After much deliberation,

Duhalde abandoned in January 2002 the fixed one-to-one peso—dollar parity that had been in place for 10 years. In a matter of days the peso lost a large part of its value in the unregulated market. A provisional "official" exchange rate was set at 1.4 pesos per dollar.

In addition to the corralito, *the Ministry of Economy dictated the* pesificación *(peso-ification), by which all bank accounts denominated in dollars would be converted to pesos at the official rate. This measure angered most savings holders and appeals were made by many citizens to declare it unconstitutional.*

After a few months the exchange rate was left to float more or less freely. The peso suffered a huge depreciation, which in turn prompted inflation. The economic situation became steadily worse with regard to inflation and unemployment during 2002. By that time the original one-to-one rate had skyrocketed to nearly 4 pesos per dollar, while the accumulated inflation since the devaluation was about 80 percent. The quality of life of the average Argentine was lowered proportionally; many businesses closed or went bankrupt, many imported products became virtually inaccessible, and salaries were left as they had been before the crisis. Unemployment skyrocketed to 25 percent.

On May 25, 2003, President Néstor Kirchner took charge. Kirchner kept Duhalde's Minister of Economy, Roberto Lavagna, in his post. Roberto Lavagna's unorthodox methods of getting Argentina out of the recession seemed to work. The government encouraged import substitution and accessible credit for businesses, staged an aggressive plan to improve tax collection, and set aside large amounts of money for social welfare, while controlling expenditure in other fields.

As a result of the administration's productive model and controlling measures (selling reserve dollars in the public market), the peso slowly revalued, reaching a three-to-one rate to the dollar. Agricultural exports grew and tourism returned.

Argentina has managed to return to growth with surprising strength; the GDP jumped 8.8 percent in 2003, 9.0 percent in 2004, 9.2 percent in 2005, 8.5 percent in 2006, and 8.7 percent in 2007. Although average wages have increased 17 percent annually since 2002 (jumping 25 percent from that year to May 2008), consumer prices have partly accompanied this surge.

During the economic collapse many business owners and foreign investors drew all their money out of the Argentine economy and sent it overseas. As a result many small and medium enterprises closed due to lack of capital, thereby exacerbating unemployment. Many workers at these enterprises, faced with a sudden loss of employment and no source of income, decided to reopen businesses on their own, without the presence of the owners and their capital, as self-managed cooperatives.

"In Buenos Aires in 1985, it was no longer possible to buy anything at night for what it had cost in the morning." —Writer Osval do Soriano

ARGENTINA IN THE NEW MILLENNIUM

Argentina faces many difficult decisions in its efforts to sustain strong social programs while producing goods that can compete in the modern global economy.

In the 1990s Argentina suffered some severe economic crises. In 1991 the Menem administration tied the local currency, the peso, to the U.S. dollar, which meant that 1 peso would be worth 1 U.S. dollar. The government also limited the amount of money circulating by tying it to real reserves held by the national bank. This was done in an effort to stop the country's high inflation rate.

Although the Menem government succeeded in lowering Argentina's inflation rate, the country was severely affected by the economic crisis in Mexico in 1995 and anxiety about the fate of Brazil's economy, the region's largest, in 1998. These events provoked rising interest rates and capital flight from Argentina, as many citizens and private companies lost confidence in the country's economy. As a consequence they withdrew their savings and deposited them in overseas banks. In 1999 after sustained blows, the Argentine GDP showed a negative 3 percent growth rate.

De la Rúa, who took office in 1999, inherited an ailing economy with a foreign debt totaling $149 billion, or 2.5 percent of the annual GDP. De la Rúa made a deal with the IMF for a $7.4 billion loan to help pay Argentina's debts. His team then embarked on a path of trade liberalization, deregulation, and privatization. But external economic shocks and failures of the system caused the economy to crumble slowly and in 2002, Argentina officially defaulted on $132 billion of its debt, and the peg of the Argentine peso to the U.S. dollar was officially scrapped.

A measure of financial stability returned after 2002, and the Argentine economy grew again with surprising strength: 9 percent annual growth, sustained for five consecutive years (between 2003 and 2007). This stability was initially due to a surge in trade surpluses and increase in business investment. The global recession of 2007 to 2010 affected the economy in 2009, with growth slowing to 0.8 percent. High economic growth resumed in 2010, and GDP expanded by 8.5 percent. However, growth has been shadowed by inflation, which the opposition claims the government has been underreporting. Official statistics put inflation at 10.9 percent; observers claim inflation is much higher, at 25 to 30 percent in 2010.

INTERNET LINKS

www.indexmundi.com/argentina/economy_profile.html

This site provides concise information and an excellent overview of the Argentine economy.

http://topdocumentaryfilms.com/argentinas-economic-collapse/

This site contains factual documentary on the Argentinean economic collapse in 12 parts.

www.doingbusiness.org/data/exploreeconomies/argentina

This site provides rankings and information on doing business in Argentina. It also includes a downloadable economic profile of Argentina.

In 2005, for the first time since the 2001 collapse, the banking system made a profit.

ENVIRONMENT

A colony of Magellanic penguins by the shore in Patagonia, near Antarctica. The species is classified as "threatened," primarily due to oil spills and climate change, which has displaced nearby fish populations, so the penguins swim an extra 50 miles (80.4 km) farther while their mates are sitting on the nest and starving.

5

A MODERN, INDUSTRIALIZED country, Argentina faces a number of environmental challenges. The air in the big cities is polluted by motor vehicle emissions and industrial waste, while soil farming areas are slowly being eroded from intense farming. Many Argentines have pressured the government to agree to and comply with a number of international agreements to protect the natural environment at home and abroad.

The environment in Argentina is characterized by high biodiversity, breathtaking natural beauty, and abundant resources.

The arid badlands of the Valle de la Luna, or "Valley of the Moon," at the Ischigualasto Provincial Park in La Rioja.

The major environmental issues in Argentina are pollution and the loss of agricultural lands. The soil is threatened by erosion, salinization, and deforestation. Air pollution is also a problem due to chemical agents from industrial sources. The water supply is threatened by the uncontrolled dumping of pesticides, hydrocarbons, and heavy metals.

NATURAL WEALTH

One of the largest countries in the world, spanning a few climatic zones and ecosystems, Argentina has a wealth of biodiversity and natural beauty. The Argentine climate and landscape vary from subtropical in the north to subantarctic in the south, from rainy coasts and river-fed plains in the east to dry semi-deserts and mountains in the west.

Monkey puzzle trees in the ancient forest of Lanin National Park in the Neuquén Province. The park houses forests of diverse tree varieties, many species of which are not found anywhere else in Argentina.

Across these regions live many different species of plants, including grasslands in the Pampas, virgin rain forests in the north, flowering cacti in the Chaco semi-desert of the northwest, and thorn forests and monkey puzzle forests in the south. The monkey puzzle tree is an evergreen tree growing to 130 feet (40 m) tall with a trunk that can reach 7 feet (2 m) in diameter. In addition to its diverse flora, Argentina is also home to some of the continent's most amazing animals. The Pampas and Patagonia regions are home to several kinds of hoofed animals, including the wild boar, axis deer, fallow deer, red deer, mouflon, wild goat, and black antelope. River-dwelling mammals include the giant Brazilian otter and marine otter. The mountain lion, or puma, makes its home in the mountains, whereas armadillos inhabit the plains. Coastal waters host a variety of sea creatures, such as whales, seals, and penguins.

Habitat destruction is probably the single greatest threat to Argentina's wildlife. Human settlement and farming have caused serious damage to the

DESERTIFICATION IN THE GRAN CHACO

In Argentina's northwest, near the border with Bolivia and Paraguay, economic pressures are destroying both the natural environment and cultural diversity. This area is part of the Gran Chaco, a semiarid region with low rainfall and few waterways. The Gran Chaco is home to indigenous peoples, who have learned to survive under conditions of intense heat and water scarcity, through gardening, gathering, hunting, and fishing. One of the indigenous groups, the Wichí have been active in letting the world know about the destruction of their environment.

Recently, due to pressure from the government to increase the production of beef, ranchers have begun to move their herds deeper into the Gran Chaco. Cattle are not indigenous to the environment, and as they graze, they destroy local plant life, stripping the land of its

natural vegetation and leaving it exposed to the heat of the sun. Fewer plants survive as the ground becomes harder and drier. This hardening and drying of the ground is called desertification.

The Wichí are petitioning the provincial government in Salta to recognize their claim on the land and to protect the land from further damage. If the area is developed without careful environmental planning, the Wichí may lose their land and their culture.

natural environment. In the north cattle ranchers have destroyed grassland areas to make way for pastures. In the south sheep farming has encroached on natural habitats.

Threatened species in Argentina include 32 types of mammals, 55 species of birds, 5 types of reptiles, 30 species of amphibians, 12 species of fish, and 42 species of plants. Birds make up the majority of the threatened species. Birds suffer the most when forests are cut down to make way for towns. The

list of endangered birds reads like a collection of paint colors: purple-barred ground dove, red-spectacled parrot, blue-throated macaw, purple-bellied parrot, ochre-breasted pipet, and saffron-cowled blackbird.

The southern river otter and marine otter are at risk of extinction, as are the giant armadillo and lesser fairy armadillo. Off the coast, the blue, rorqual, and finback whales are also in need of protection.

A southern right whale and its calf swim through the Atlantic coast of the Península Valdés. This important nature reserve was listed by UNESCO as a World Heritage Site in 1999.

PLANTS AND ANIMALS OF ARGENTINA

EARLIEST LAND PLANTS FOUND IN ARGENTINA The earliest plants to grow on land have been discovered in Argentina. The discovery puts back by 10 million years the colonization of land by plants and suggests that a diversity of land plants had evolved by 472 million years ago. The newly found plants are liverworts, very simple plants that lack stems or roots. They were discovered in the Río Capillas, in the Sierras Subandinas in the Central Andean Basin of northwest Argentina. The previous record holder of the earliest known land plants were small liverwort cryptospores found in Saudi Arabia and the Czech Republic.

THE RORQUAL WHALE Rorqual whales include the largest animal that has ever lived, the blue whale, which can reach 165 tons (150 metric tons), and two others that easily pass 55 tons (50 metric tons). Even the smallest of the group, the northern minke whale, reaches 10 tons (9 metric tons).

Rorquals are slender and streamlined in shape, and most have narrow, elongated flippers. They have a dorsal fin, situated far back on the body, near to the tail. Rorquals feed by gulping in water, and then pushing it out through their baleen plates with their tongue. They feed on crustaceans, such as krill, and also on various fish, such as herrings and sardines.

Most rorquals breed in temperate waters during the winter, and then migrate back to the polar feeding grounds rich in plankton and krill for the short polar summer.

EMPEROR PENGUIN The emperor penguin is the tallest and heaviest of all living penguin species and is native to Antarctica. The male and female penguins are similar in plumage and size, reaching 48 inches (122 cm) in height and weighing anywhere from 49 to 99 pounds (22 to 45 kg). The dorsal side and head are black and sharply delineated from the white belly, pale-yellow breast, and bright yellow ear patches. Like all penguins it is flightless, with a streamlined body, and wings stiffened and flattened into flippers for a marine habitat.

The emperor penguin is perhaps best known for the sequence of journeys adults make each year to mate and to feed their offspring. The only penguin species that breeds during the Antarctic winter, it treks 31—75 miles (50—120 km) over the ice to breeding colonies that may include thousands of individuals. The female lays a single egg, which is incubated by the male, while the female returns to the sea to feed; parents subsequently take turns foraging at sea and caring for their chick in the colony. The lifespan is typically 20 years in the wild.

The emperor penguin is the tallest and heaviest of all living penguin species and is endemic, or native, to Antarctica.

POLLUTION

As Argentina's largest city, Buenos Aires has not been able to escape the scourge of air pollution that afflicts most cities once they reach a certain population size. Buenos Aires is now home to 13 million people, 4 million more than the population of New York City. Buenos Aires is blessed to be situated on a vast flat plain right next to the La Plata River system and is frequently buffeted by moderate to strong and gusty winds throughout most of the summer. These winds combined with the flat terrain prevent the accumulation of air pollution.

However, more could certainly be done. Vehicles are not required to be fitted with catalytic converters, so nitrous oxide emission from vehicles is extremely high during peak driving hours. There was once a freaky event where winds blew smog from burning pastures over Buenos Aires in 2008; however, such occurrences are extremely rare.

ENVIRONMENTAL PROTECTION EFFORTS

Argentina is a signatory to a number of international accords that aim to protect the world's natural heritage. Argentina recognizes recommendations set out in international protocols on biodiversity, climate change, endangered species, hazardous waste, marine dumping, the nuclear test ban, ozone layer protection, and whaling, for example. In addition the Argentine government has set aside more than 20 national parks in an effort to protect fragile environments. One of these, Península Valdés in Patagonia, has been designated a World Heritage Site by the United Nations. Península Valdés has been declared a site for the preservation of marine mammals. Southern elephant seals, sea lions, southern right whales, and orcas breed in and around the peninsula.

Argentina has also been active in protecting the Earth's ozone layer. The country is a world leader in setting voluntary targets for reducing greenhouse gas emissions such as carbon monoxide.

MARINE CONSERVATION

Dr. Patricia Gandini, president of Argentina's National Park Administration, announced four new marine protected areas (MPAs) on October 27, 2010. These will cover more than 1,435,188 acres (580,800 ha) of the southwest Atlantic Ocean, extending along Argentina's coast. This will bring the total area of marine protected areas in Argentina to 3,362,610 acres (1,360,800 ha) and is in line with the country's aim to establish an effectively managed, fully representative network of MPAs spanning 24,710,538 acres (10,000,000 ha)—more than 10 percent of the country's waters. The new MPAs are areas of high biodiversity value and have species such as the jackass penguin, the southern elephant seal, and the southern right whale.

THE *CARTONEROS* OF BUENO AIRES

A daily sight in Buenos Aires around dusk are the legions of cartoneros—*the poor, often foreign (Bolivian, Paraguayan) families who come into the city center and residential neighborhoods to pick through trash for cardboard (*cartón*), paper, plastic, and glass. From the outskirts they often enter via the* tren blanco *(the "white train," a commuter train stripped of seats for this purpose), whereas those who live in the* villas miserias *(misery villages) pay a peso or so for a crew boss with a pickup truck to drive them.*

Statistics on cartoneros *and recycling:*

- *Some 400,000 tons of cardboard and plastic are collected and sold annually.*
- Cartoneros *earn 70 million pesos annually selling cardboard and plastic.*
- *By the time these materials are passed through middlemen and back into business, they are sold for 450 million pesos.*
- *There are 20,000* cartoneros *today, compared to 40,000 just after the 2001 financial crisis.*
- *A total of 10,500 of the* cartoneros *are officially registered with the government.*

Cartoneros get 0.20 pesos/pound (0.45 pesos/kg) for white paper, 0.08—0.09 pesos for cardboard, 0.05 pesos for newsprint, 0.25—0.30 pesos for plastic bottles, and 0.07—0.10 pesos for glass. The neighborhood bosses who collect from the cartoneros *add 20 percent to the price before they sell the bulk to larger recycling collectors, who add another 100 percent before they sell it to paper mills as raw material, who themselves sextuple (multiply by 6) the price when they turn it into finished products that they sell into the public market.*

Eloísa Cartonera is a nonprofit, social, and community-related artistic project settled in Buenos Aries, which produces handmade books with cardboard covers. The organization purchases this cardboard from cartoneros. *The covers are painted by hand, with tempera paints and paintbrushes. Eloísa has a catalog of authors who are renowned worldwide: Ricardo Piglia, Cesar Aira, Gonzalo Milan (Chile), Luis Chavez (Costa Rica), and many others. The project publishes previously unpublished literature by these famous authors.*

UNESCO WORLD HERITAGE SITES IN ARGENTINA

IGUAZÚ NATIONAL PARK This national park of 212 square miles (550 square km) contains the Iguazú Falls, one of the great national beauties of Argentina, and the subtropical jungle. The fauna of the park includes several endangered species, such as the jaguar, South American tapir, and ocelot. One can also find birds such as swifts and large toucans. There is a wide variety of butterflies here as well.

The Iguazú River ends in the Paraná River 14.3 miles (23 km) beyond the falls, after a 820-mile (1,320-km) course. Inside the park the river goes up to 1,640 yards (1,500 m) wide and turns first south, then north, forming a large U-shape. Its banks are densely populated by trees, including the ceibo (cockspur coral tree), whose flower is Argentina's national flower.

TALAMPAYA NATIONAL PARK Talampaya National Park is located in the center of La Rioja province. It was designated a provincial reserve in 1975, a national park in 1997, and a UNESCO World Heritage Site in 2000.

The park covers an area of 830 square miles (2,150 square km), at an altitude of 4,921 feet (1,500 m) above sea level. Its purpose is to protect important archaeological and paleontological sites found in the area.

The park includes the following:
- the dry bed of the Talampaya River, where dinosaurs lived millions of years ago, and where fossils have been found;
- the Talampaya gorge and its rock formations with walls up to 469 feet (143 m) high, narrowing to 262 feet (80 m) at one point;
- the remains of indigenous settlements, such as the petroglyphs of the Puerta del Cañón;
- a botanical garden of local flora at the narrow point of the canyon;
- regional fauna, including guanacos, hares, maras, foxes, and condors.

LOS GLACIARES NATIONAL PARK Parque Nacional Los Glaciares is a national park in the Santa Cruz province, in Patagonia. It consists of an area of 1,722 square miles (4,459 square km) and is the second-largest national park in Argentina. In 1981 it was declared a World Heritage Site by UNESCO.

Its name refers to the giant ice cap in the Andes range that feeds 47 large glaciers, of which only 13 flow toward the Atlantic Ocean. The ice cap is the largest outside of Antarctica and Greenland. In other parts of the world, glaciers start at a height of at least 8,202 feet (2,500 m) above mean sea level, but due to the size of the ice cap, these glaciers begin at only 4,921 feet (1,500 m), sliding down to 656 feet (200 m), eroding the surface of the mountains that support them.

Los Glaciares, of which 30 percent is covered by ice, can be divided into two parts, each corresponding to one of the two elongated big lakes partially contained in the park. Lake Argentino, 566 square miles (1,466 square km), the largest in Argentina, is in the south, whereas Lake Viedma, 425 square miles (1,100 square km), is in the north. Both lakes feed the Santa Cruz River that flows down to Puerto Santa Cruz on the Atlantic Ocean.

The northern half consists of part of Viedma Lake, the Viedma Glacier, and a few minor glaciers. The southern part has the major glaciers that flow into Lake Argentino: Perito Moreno Glacier, Upsala Glacier, and Spegazzini Glacier. Typical excursion boats travel between icebergs to visit Bahía Onelli, and the otherwise inaccessible Spegazzini and Upsala. The Perito Moreno is reachable by land.

The mountains hold most of the humidity from the Pacific Ocean, letting through only the ice coldness (annual average of 45.5°F [7.5°C]) and creating an arid steppe on the Argentine side of the range. This area is a habitat for the guanaco, cougar, and gray fox.

The Talampaya National Park is named after the Quechua "dry riverbed of the Tala (tree)," because of the water erosion from the Talampaya River which created the park's signature underground sandstone canyons.

ANTARCTICA

Argentina, along with Australia, Chile, France, New Zealand, Norway, and the United Kingdom, claims territory in Antarctica. All seven nations, along with 35 others, signed the Antarctic Treaty in 1959. The treaty took effect in 1961 and was strengthened in 1991 by the Protocol on Environmental Protection, which defines the Antarctica as a "natural reserve devoted to peace and science."

- *It is the highest continent in the world, with an average elevation of 7,550 feet (2,300 m).*

- *It is the size of the United States and Mexico combined, with 5.4 million square miles (14 million square km) of territory.*

- *The diameter of the continent is 3,450 miles (5,551 km), or about the distance between Los Angeles and New York.*

- *The coastline is 19,800 miles (31,858 km) long, or about the distance from Anchorage, Alaska, to the southernmost tip of Chile.*

- *There is no vegetation whatsoever; 98 percent of the continent is ice throughout the year, whereas 2 percent is barren rock.*

- *The ice packs and frigid waters are home to the emperor penguin, the largest of penguins, weighing up to 65 pounds (30 kg) and standing more than 3 feet (90 cm) tall.*

Only a few scientific research teams are allowed at any one time to live in Antarctica, the world's largest protected nature reserve. Of the countries that send out research teams to the Antarctica, Argentina maintains the greatest number of science stations, with six year-round stations and seven summer stations.

Understanding Antarctica is critical to understanding global climate changes because it is over this continent that scientists have discovered the thinning of the atmospheric layer called the ozone.

HOPE FOR TOMORROW

Protecting the environment is not limited to passing laws or even setting aside nature reserves, but these are essential first steps. Argentina has led the way among South American countries in taking these first steps and in trying to protect its natural heritage. Argentina is also a world leader in setting voluntary greenhouse gas emission targets. The country's greatest challenge today, however, lies in finding a balance between meeting its needs for economic growth and preserving its natural environment.

"Years pass and our lands become impoverished, because the people who have come from the outside to occupy them know not how to manage them. Years pass and we become poorer." —Quoted in a Wichí (native Argentinean tribe) appeal for international support

INTERNET LINKS

www.losglaciares.com/en/index.html

This site will tell you everything you ever wanted to know about this breathtaking national park.

www.iguazuargentina.com/english/

This is the official website of Iguazú National Park, with breathtaking pictures.

www.welcomeargentina.com/paseos/parque_talampaya/index_i.html

This is the website showcasing Talampaya National Park, including many impressive images.

ARGENTINES

Predominantly European features characterize

T HE HEART OF ARGENTINA is its people. Argentina has a population of 41.8 million people. The typical Argentine does not look particularly "South American." The high cheekbones, darker skin tones, and coal black hair of the indigenous Indians and the mestizos and mulattos (people of mixed black and white ancestry) are not characteristic of the crowds on Argentina's streets. Most Argentines look European.

6

Argentina is a melting pot of different people and is often referred to as a "crucible of races."

Gauchos, or Argentinean cowboys, at an ranch near San Antonio de Areco. The gauchos embody the essential Argentine qualities of nobility, courage, and independence.

Most Latin American countries have large populations of mestizos and people of African descent. In contrast most Argentines—97 percent—are of European—mostly Italian and Spanish—descent. The remaining 3 percent are mestizo, Indian, and other groups.

As large numbers of Europeans migrated to Argentina, they tended to form their own neighborhoods. Buenos Aires and other large cities still have ethnic neighborhoods, where the special foods and traditions of different European countries are preserved. Some of these groups publish newspapers in their own languages. They also run schools, hospitals, and clubs that are mainly targeted at members of their ethnic group but are often open to all other members of society.

Argentina's largest ethnic group is the Italian community. About four out of ten people in Argentina are of Italian descent, whereas about three out of ten trace their heritage back to Spain. Most of the Italian immigrants have settled in and around Buenos Aires. Italian settlement in Argentina, along with Spanish settlement, forms the backbone of today's Argentine society. Argentine culture has significant connections to Italian culture, also in terms of language, customs, and traditions.

Argentina's population consists mostly of people from different European countries, such as Italy, Spain, France, Britain, Russia, Germany, and Poland.

OTHER ETHNIC ROOTS

Argentina once had the largest British community outside of Great Britain. British expatriates were influential in the developing of Argentina's railway, telephone, electricity, gas, and steamship services. They brought sports such as soccer, rugby, cricket, polo, and tennis. They even imported cattle from England. Their descendants are called Anglo-Argentines. The Falklands War between Argentina and Great Britain presented them with a potential conflict of loyalties, but most sided with Argentina.

Women living in a slum in Buenos Aires. Since the 1930s, large numbers of people have left the countryside to seek work in the larger cities. Many found only part-time work and have become part of a poor lower class living in slum conditions.

In addition more than one million Europeans came to Argentina following World War II. Europe's loss was Argentina's gain. Along with the numerous Italian, Spanish, English, and Welsh immigrants, Argentina was also enriched by people of Austrian, Dutch, French, German, Irish, Jewish, Polish, Swiss, Russian, Portuguese, Chinese, Japanese, and Syrian descent. Immigrants have also come from neighboring South American countries, largely for political or economic reasons. More recently newcomers have arrived from Korea and Southeast Asia.

SOCIAL CLASSES

From the mid-18th to the mid-19th century, political and social life in Argentina was shaped by the landed aristocracy—the big rural landowners. Many had close ties with Great Britain and its culture. Members of the upper class considered themselves among the world's most sophisticated people.

When the major waves of European immigrants arrived in Argentina in the late 1800s, they found that the rural areas were controlled by the landed aristocracy. The newcomers could not easily own land or houses in the countryside, so they settled in the cities, especially in Buenos Aires.

The Japanese-Argentine population has assimilated well into Argentine society, and most of them speak Spanish instead of Japanese.

A gaucho showing off his belt. Argentine gauchos are known around the world for their thick leather belts, decorated with silver pieces and sometimes old silver coins.

Argentina's large and prosperous cities enabled immigrants to find jobs and education and become part of the middle class. The urban middle class today includes workers in small businesses as well as government officials and professionals.

In the past the landed aristocracy held most of the political power. Today leaders in industry and commerce, military officers, and professionals exercise considerable power in determining how the country is run. As is the case in many other countries, social classes in Argentina are still largely based on money, education, and family background.

Among the wealthy are ranchers, or *estancieros* (es-tahn-see-EH-ros), who own large estates and herds of cattle in the country, but who reside in the cities. They work their farms and ranches with their families and with the help of hired hands.

THE PROUD GAUCHOS

The gauchos of the past were a special group of Argentine men—mostly mestizos—who roamed the Pampas on horseback. They have become folk heroes, inspiring Argentines even today, as symbols of strength and individualism. A much smaller number of gauchos still work on cattle ranches in Argentina.

Like the cowboys of the North American West, the legendary gauchos were excellent horsemen. They tamed wild horses, herded cattle, and exhibited their skill and courage in everything they did. They could find their way on the plains under any circumstances. By chewing grass, they could tell whether there was water nearby and whether it was salt water or fresh. They could tell directions from the lay of the grass and count the number of riders by the sound of the horses' hooves.

The gauchos often led rugged lives with few comforts. They lived in small homes with mud walls and floors, a straw roof, and no windows. The gauchos were proud, self-reliant, and tough. They fought for survival against the

forces of nature and against invaders. During colonial times they opposed the authority of Spain. Later they lived in opposition to the new settlers who fenced in the open range.

During the 19th century the gauchos' main job was the transportation of cattle to the markets in Buenos Aires. The building of roads and railroads and the fencing in of the estancias (ranches) changed the traditional role of the gauchos. Although fewer in number, they still work on the Pampas, driving tractors, repairing engines, and vaccinating cattle.

The traditional gauchos adopted the use of bolas, also known as boleadoras, from the indigenous Indians. A bola is a long rope with two or three ends tied to hard balls covered with leather. Bolas were used for fighting and hunting, especially the pursuit of the rhea, a bird similar to the ostrich. When thrown at a running target, the bola wraps itself around the legs, tripping the animal and tying its legs. Gauchos still exhibit their legendary horsemanship skills at rodeos.

The gauchos of the past survived on a diet of meat and yerba mate, a holly tea. A typical picture of a gaucho shows him on horseback or at rest, singing and strumming a guitar or sipping yerba mate from a hollowed-out gourd through a metal straw.

A gaucho on horseback in Estancia San Isidro del Llano. The hat and jacket shield the gaucho from glaring sunlight and protect him from the cold.

DISAPPEARANCE OF AFRO-ARGENTINES

Argentina had a significant African population in its early years as a republic. Afro-Argentines were the descendants of slaves imported from Africa by the Spanish in the 16th century. Around 1778 Afro-Argentines constituted about 30 percent of Buenos Aires' population.

Slave trade was outlawed in 1813, and most slaves were freed by 1827. A few, however, did not attain freedom until 1861. After Argentina's independence, most Afro-Argentines continued to suffer discrimination in Argentine society.

Between 1836 and 1887 the percentage of Afro-Argentines in Buenos Aires dropped from 26 percent to 1.8 percent. Historical paintings, prints, and photographs as well as the epic poem Martín Fierro *depict Afro-Argentines. Descendants of Afro-Argentines constitute 4 percent of the Argentine population today. During the wars of independence (1810—21) and the War of the Triple Alliance (1865—70), the male cohort within this ethnic group was reduced when thousands of black citizens were forcefully recruited and used as front-line soldiers; most of the remainder were absorbed by intermarriage into the general population. Some researchers argue that rather than decrease there was a process of "invisibility" of the Afro Argentine population and their cultural roots.*

THE CRIOLLOS

The early criollos have been credited with giving the Argentine people the traits of strong national pride, independence, warm hospitality, and courteous manners.

In colonial times criollos were people born to Spanish parents in Argentina. Later the word was used to describe the descendants of the early Spanish settlers, as opposed to the descendants of later waves of European immigrants. Today the term *criollo* is also used to describe a person who lives in the country or in a small town.

INDIGENOUS ARGENTINES

The small minority of pure indigenous Argentines lives mostly in the isolated areas of the Andes Mountains, the Gran Chaco, Patagonia, and Tierra del Fuego. The Diaguita Indians, for example, live west of Salta at an altitude of 9,800 feet (2,987 m). This area was part of the Incan empire before the Spaniards arrived in South America in the 16th century.

Although the soil is poor, the indigenous Indians farm the mountainsides, growing beans, corn, and potatoes. They use irrigation channels built centuries ago by their Inca ancestors to help in their farming.

Because the air is too thin at this altitude for cattle and sheep to live, the indigenous Indians use llamas for meat, wool, and transportation. From llama wool the women weave clothing for their families. They also use the wool to make socks, sweaters, scarves, and blankets, which they sell to tourists.

Each indigenous community has its own distinctive style of dressing. Women's hairstyles also differ depending on the region. Most Argentine Indians follow a mix of indigenous and European traditions. Although they may profess to be Christians, many still pray to the gods of the sun, moon, earth, thunder, rain, and lightning.

Today there are about 700,000 indigenous people, representing 1.7 percent of the Argentine population.

INTERNET LINKS

www.argbrit.org/

This online museum depicts what it was like to be a British settler in Argentina in the 19th century. It includes drawings and newspaper articles from as far back as 1807.

www.travelsur.net/gauchos.htm

Learn all about the gauchos, the Argentine cowboys. Seeing how they turned their image from one that was disdained to one that is favored by Argentine society is particularly interesting. The six video files of gaucho dances at the bottom of the page are fascinating.

www.library.nd.edu/rarebooks/exhibits/riverplate/08-gauchos/index.shtml

This site provides a description of the evolution of the gauchos from the first Spanish settlers to today.

LIFESTYLE

The Galerias Pacifico shopping mall in Calle Florida in Buenos Aires. Most Argentines are very fashion-conscious. Many shops in fashionable districts sell European and American brand goods.

7

A RGENTINE SOCIETY IS DYNAMIC and evolving, a colorful blend of indigenous and imported cultures. Many Argentines follow customs and traditions brought by their ancestors from their country of origin.

Argentina's great geographical diversity has also shaped different lifestyles in different regions. The Welsh sheep-ranchers of Patagonia, the indigenous Indian farmers of the Andes, and the city dwellers of Buenos Aires lead entirely different lives.

Yet certain customs and traits are shared by most Argentines: They are strongly nationalistic; they are passionate about the arts; and they love to talk about sports, especially soccer, and politics.

FROM BIRTH TO DEATH

The majority of Argentines is made up of Roman Catholics, and they follow the traditional practices of the Church to mark important events in their lives. Argentines also follow traditions common to Latin American countries. Children are usually baptized as infants, and they celebrate their First Communion at the age of 8. Girls follow the Latin American tradition of celebrating their 15th birthday with a big dance party. This event marks a girl's induction into society.

When a couple gets engaged, they first exchange rings. The woman wears her ring on the fourth finger of her right hand until the wedding, when she shifts it to her left hand. In the wedding ceremony the groom walks in with his mother and the bride with her father. This custom symbolizes that both are leaving their families and joining as husband and wife at the altar.

"The Argentines are still trying to figure out if they're European or Latin American, and they are famous throughout Latin America for not having made up their minds yet." —Deirdre Ball, author of *Insight Guide, Argentina*

Locals crossing a busy street in the city of Buenos Aires.

When people die, their bodies may be either buried or cremated. It is unusual for the body of a dead person to be embalmed and viewed in an open coffin, as was done for Evita Perón after her death.

FAMILY LIFE

Family life is very important to most of the Argentines. Family members tend to be nurturing and supportive of one another, and Argentines love to hear compliments about their home and children. A close bond among family members makes them fiercely loyal to one another.

Children are rarely sent away to boarding school; they are quite likely to live at home until marriage and then settle near their parents. University students generally attend classes in their hometown and continue to live with their parents. Workers often come home for lunch.

Argentines care for their elderly parents and frequently invite a widowed parent to live with them. It is not common for the elderly to live in nursing homes.

The extended family of aunts, uncles, and cousins gathers often. This family network is valuable, as gaining entrance into good schools and getting a job are often made possible by family connections.

The father is often a strong, authoritarian figure in the family. Traditionally he also bears the responsibility of earning enough money to support the family, although women also work and contribute to the family's income.

Young people live by the rules of their families and are influenced by family members through their adolescence and often until after marriage.

CITY LIFESTYLE

The history of Argentina is marked by a long conflict between the city and the countryside. To this day urban and rural Argentines have contrasting lifestyles.

City life in Argentina reflects the strong influence of the European immigrants. The city plan—the layout of streets, parks, and squares—and architecture of Buenos Aires have a European look. As in Spanish cities, the cathedral and chief government buildings are found facing the plaza or main square. Argentina's artistic culture, education, fashion, business etiquette, and rules of behavior are also distinctly European.

The Buenos Aires *porteños* are the elite of Argentina. They dominate the government and cultural life of the country. *Porteños* tend to view themselves as more sophisticated and well informed about world affairs. They set trends in behavior and fashion that spread to the provinces. Many *porteños* have little interest in visiting other parts of Argentina. They are sometimes accused of having a superior attitude toward Argentines living outside of Buenos Aires and of viewing non-*porteños*—even those living in cities—as campesinos, or country folk.

A farmer driving a tractor on his farm in Lujan de Cuyo.

COUNTRY LIFESTYLE

In the countryside the European influence on lifestyles is less noticeable. Rural Argentines lead different lifestyles according to their economic status. Rich country people live and work on huge ranches, often built as luxurious country estates. Others live on small farms. The poorest people live in homes made of straw and mud with dirt floors.

FRIENDSHIP THRIVES IN THE CAFÉ

Argentines love to discuss sports, politics, philosophy, and the arts. In Buenos Aires, particularly, having discussions means lingering in a café talking with friends. There are hundreds of old cafés lining the busy streets of Buenos Aires. The most important feature of a café is its relaxed atmosphere; the meals served are considered much less important. The waiters are trained never to rush customers. The English custom of having tea and snacks in the afternoon lives on in Argentina.

Founded in 1858 the Tortoni is the oldest café in Buenos Aires. It has a charming old billiard room, and the walls are decorated with souvenirs from the many painters and writers who have gathered there over the years. Conspirators and army chiefs have also gone to sip coffee or play a game of chess. Jazz performances add to the atmosphere on weekends.

Because Argentines are often creatures of habit, many prefer to meet over and over again at the same café. The favorite discussion is what it means to be Argentine.

Cafés, restaurants, and clubs stay open very late. The typical workday runs from 9:00 A.M. to 7:00 P.M., though sometimes it may extend as late as 10:00 P.M. It is not uncommon for Argentines to have dinner as late as 10:00 P.M. or even midnight. Famous for nightlife, some streets of Buenos Aires are bustling with people long after the clock strikes midnight.

Rural Argentines tend to see themselves as being more humble, having more common sense, and being in better touch with the land than people in the cities. They sometimes resent what appears to them to be the arrogance of the *porteños*.

The great rivalry between Argentines of the countryside and the people of Buenos Aires, once very heated, no longer erupts into violence. The two different ways of life are today increasingly seen as complementary to each other.

RICH AND POOR

Economic problems in past decades have widened the social gap between the rich and the poor in Argentina, creating vast differences in lifestyle between the wealthy of Buenos Aires' northern suburbs and the poor of the slums known as *villas miserias* (VEE-jahs mee-SEH-ree-ahs). Sometimes the two live only a bus stop away from each other.

In recent years church and volunteer organizations have joined efforts to raise money to build adequate housing for the shanty town residents of Tigre, a fading resort northwest of the city.

One stumbling block for these organizations is the unwillingness of Argentines to give money to charity, as there have been cases in the past of mismanagement of funds by charitable organizations.

POLITICAL TALK

Under the democratic governments, the Argentine people have gained the right to voice their political views without fear.

In 1945 thousands of workers answered Evita Perón's call to protest her husband's detention by marching in the Plaza de Mayo. Historians mark this event as the day the working class gained real political power.

Street rallies, marches, and people carrying placards on the streets are the traditional ways in which Argentines express their political opinions. Traffic halts for union demonstrators and students singing songs of protest. Political graffiti can be found on many buildings and walls.

Argentina's social divide shows in the contrast between a slum home and the towering city skyscapers in the background.

THE SUGAR, SALT, AND SPICE OF RELATIONSHIPS

The warmth Argentines show to their family members is often extended to friends. Argentines tend to make physical contact when greeting. They hug and kiss when they meet and when they leave one another. When introduced, men shake hands, but close male friends may hug one another. Women friends shake hands and kiss one another on one cheek.

Flirting has a certain style in Argentina. A man may pass a woman on the street and compliment her on her beauty without expecting her to stop or reply. His compliment, called a piropo *(pee-ROH-poh), may be indirect, such as: "It must be lonely in heaven since one of the more beautiful angels descended to Earth!" Less poetically, when passing a mature woman, a man might say: "Old but still good."*

Women also flirt, making witty remarks and even put-downs that are meant to be heard and enjoyed by their friends. In the words of a common Argentine saying, "In the United States, women are called sweet; in Spain, they are called salty; but in Argentina, women are spicy."

During elections Argentines turn out in large numbers to vote at the polls. Most speak freely about which political party they support and whom they voted for in the last elections.

WOMEN

Traditionally Argentine women did not play a large role in public life. Evita Perón was the first woman to advocate and promote women's rights in Argentina. She is still admired by many feminists for her active role in politics. Evita worked to gain women working benefits and the right to vote.

Argentine men and women have equal rights under the constitution. Since the 1940s women have become more active in professional jobs. Evita Perón was extremely influential in her husband's administration, and Perón's third wife, Isabel, became president of the country. An increasing number of women also work as doctors, lawyers, and architects, among other professions. Through Evita's efforts, divorce was legalized, but this

Many visitors praise the friendliness and the unpretentiousness of the Argentines. Whether you ask an owner of a large villa or a peasant for directions, the answer is always a smile and a helping hand to guide you along the way.

act was reversed shortly after her husband's fall in 1955. Divorce was not legalized again until 1987.

Women became forceful in public life during the "dirty war" when the courageous "Mothers of the Plaza de Mayo" marched past the Casa Rosada every Thursday, carrying placards inscribed with the names of their missing loved ones. At great personal risk, they demonstrated to end human rights abuses and hold the government accountable for the "disappeared."

Today, there are large numbers of women are working in business and government, closing the professional gap between men and women, which was prevalent in Argentina until recent years. Of course, now that the president of the country is a woman, women are making tremendous strides in Argentine society. Women represent 33 percent of the Argentine Congress, as opposed to 15 percent in the U.S. Congress.

Business partners going through documents. Men and women play an equal part in Argentina's modern workforce.

When a woman marries, she keeps her maiden name. If María García marries Juan Adler, she becomes María García de Adler or Señora García de Adler. Children take the father's last name. Unlike in English, letters are not addressed to "Mr. and Mrs. Juan Adler" but to "Mr. Juan Adler and Mrs.," which reads in Spanish, "Señor Juan Adler y Señora."

In the past women commonly went out accompanied by a man. This custom has changed in recent years, as active participation in business and government has given Argentine women financial and social independence.

In Argentina abuse of women is usually not brought out in the open. Crimes of rape and incest are considered shameful and frequently are not reported to doctors or the police. Although Argentina is predominantly a Catholic society, the practice of contraception and abortion is common, and there are fewer illegitimate children than in other Catholic countries.

> ## NOSTALGIA IN ARGENTINA
>
> *Argentines are said to have a sentimental streak. They remember the past in songs and stories and in the glorification of the gaucho as a folk hero. The architecture of the cities is full of reminders of the past—old fountains and wrought-iron gates. Families remember their immigrant past through collections of treasured photographs. Tango music expresses this nostalgia with lyrics that speak of lost loves and unfulfilled dreams.*

ARGENTINE ATTITUDES

During Argentina's fight for independence from Spain, many women managed their family's businesses and estates so that the men could help in the struggle. Some women provided food and nursing care to the militia, and a few were even involved in combat, although by accident. Other women raised money for support of the military efforts.

Although some Argentines like to make dramatic gestures, the general tendency is to avoid loud and unusual behavior in public. Nevertheless Argentines tend to express their emotions openly, as is typical of most Latin Americans.

A leisurely schedule governs the gathering of friends. People invited to dinner arrive 30—60 minutes after the specified time. When invited to a birthday party, guests bring gifts, which are usually opened in their presence.

Many Argentines go to psychiatrists or psychoanalysts, and many of the analysts in Spain are Argentines. Some think psychiatry is popular among Argentines because people see themselves more as individuals than as part of a group. Argentines tend to be quite concerned with their personal thoughts and feelings.

When you ask for directions on the street, an Argentine may give a detailed, possibly wrong, answer rather than admit that he or she does not know the way to your destination. Keeping up appearances is very important to some Argentines.

Some dramatize their lives or cover up their poverty with a bit of exaggeration. For example a woman may tell her friends that she was chauffeured to the restaurant where they are having lunch when she actually came on the bus. A man may tell a new acquaintance that he lives in a building known for its expensive apartments when he actually lives in a more modest home.

SOCIAL AND BUSINESS CUSTOMS

Argentines prefer to do business in person rather than over the telephone. Appointments for business meetings are preferred to unexpected visits to an office.

It is polite to make small talk at the end of a business meeting, rather than leave abruptly when things are settled. Most Argentines prefer not to discuss business during meals. The pace of negotiations is much slower than in the United States and is based more on personal contact.

On a social basis, many people drop in on friends from around 4:00 to 6:00 P.M. without calling ahead. Social plans are likely to be spontaneous, rather than scheduled weeks in advance.

In Buenos Aires, in particular, people stay out late many nights of the week and seem to survive on little sleep. Shops are closed on Saturday afternoons so that people may rest to prepare themselves for their Saturday night activities. On Sundays families gather for large noon meals. Shops are closed on Sundays.

Abortion in Argentina has remained prohibited as of 2010, and is legal only in cases of rape, or where the life of the mother in danger. However, half a million illegal abortions are performed annually in Argentina.

INTERNET LINKS

www.transitionsabroad.com/listings/living/articles/living-in-buenos-aires-argentina.shtml

This page by an expatriate woman depicts what it is like to live in Buenos Aires as a local.

http://argentina.rica24.com/en/argentina-lifestyle.html

This is an informative page on the Argentine lifestyle, mannerisms, habits, and etiquette.

http://wn.com/argentina_lifestyle

This site provides interesting and varied videos on the Argentine lifestyle and also features very amusing Argentine commercials.

RELIGION

The San Francisco church in Salta Province. Many of Argentina's oldest churches are located in the northern provinces.

ROMAN CATHOLICISM IS Argentina's official religion. The vast majority of Argentines—about 92 percent—is Catholic, but only 20 percent attend church service regularly. Even so, Argentines generally take a relaxed view toward religion—a recent survey found that 11 percent of Argentines are nonreligious despite their official religious classification. However, when the Pope visited in 1982 and again in 1987, millions showed their support by flocking to see the spiritual leader.

CHRISTIANITY

According to the constitution of 1853, the president and vice president of Argentina must be Roman Catholic. This requirement was removed from the text in the 1994 constitutional reform because the president no longer designates Argentine bishops. The government also provides some financial support to the Church. The constitution guarantees freedom of religion for all. At the same time it requires that strong relations exist between the Church and the state, but in an environment of religious pluralism and freedom. The federal government pays a salary to Roman Catholic bishops, and retired priests receive minor pensions.

Religious groups can run their own churches, hospitals, social centers, and cemeteries. Religious schools are allowed, but religion is not always

8

A majority of the population of Argentina is Roman Catholic. Pentecostal churches and traditional Protestant denominations are present in most communities. Argentina has the largest Jewish population in Latin America, about 300,000. Muslim Argentines number about 500,000 to 600,000, or approximately 1.5 percent of the population.

Pachamama worship is still widespread throughout Salta and Jujuy along with Catholic beliefs, without opposition from the Catholic bishops. Pachamama is a fertility goddess of the indigenous people in parts of Argentina, Chile, Bolivia, and Peru, who presides over planting and harvesting. Her name is sometimes translated as "Mother Earth."

taught in public schools. Religious sects can be banned by the government if they appear to threaten public order and morality. The state also subsidizes many private schools, most of which are affiliated with the Catholic Church. The total economic support for the Church by the state amounts to 12 million Argentine pesos per year (about 4 million U.S. dollars).

By law all Argentine children must be registered at birth with names found in a registry of acceptable first names. These are often, but not always, the Spanish names of Catholic saints.

Within the Catholic Church, different groups, or orders, focus on a specific type of social work. Some run hospitals and orphanages; others run schools. Some are missionaries in remote areas of the country; others do work with prisoners and juvenile delinquents.

OTHER RELIGIOUS GROUPS

About 2 percent of Argentines are Protestants. Besides Roman Catholics and Protestants, there are other Christians who belong to the Armenian, Orthodox, and Ukrainian churches. Many Jews came from Europe in the late 19th and early 20th centuries; Jews now make up about 1 percent of the Argentine population and live mostly in Buenos Aires.

Muslims, members of other religious groups, and atheists make up the remaining 5 percent of the population.

Writers have called the reverence paid to Evita Perón a kind of religious fervor. After her death President Juan Perón was unsuccessful in his attempt to have his wife declared a saint by the Catholic Church. Nevertheless her

YAMANA BELIEFS

The Yamana Indians, now extinct, were an ancient aboriginal people who lived at the southern tip of Argentina. Their stories were passed down orally, without ever being put into writing until a priest, Father Martín Gusinde, documented their legends from interviews with the last Yamana survivors in the 1920s.

One Yamana myth tells of a great flood. When the people offended Lexuwakipa, a spirit disguised as an ibis, she sent down so much snow that a huge mass of ice covered the Earth. This took place at a time when men and women were battling each other. Eventually the men won by seizing the women's secret meeting place, the source of their power.

When the snow began to melt, it flooded all the Earth. The water rose steadily and rapidly. The people struggled to save themselves. Finally only five mountain peaks remained above water. The water remained level for two full days, and then subsided. Practically all the Yamana had drowned; only a few families managed to save themselves. Once the great flood had subsided, the survivors began to rebuild their homes. But ever since, men have ruled over women.

admirers continue to place fresh flowers at her tomb every day. Believers ask her to grant them favors and to protect them from harm. Her final resting place is the Duarte family tomb.

In rural areas mestizos have mixed elements of animistic religions with Catholic practices. They pray to the spirits of nature as well as to the Christian god. They hold festivals throughout the year filled with singing and dancing dedicated to indigenous gods. Superstition blends with Christianity, as when a person makes the sign of the cross to ward off the "evil eye." Rural shrines to unofficial saints are popular pilgrimage sites in the countryside.

About six weeks before Easter, just before the fasting period of Lent, the yearly celebration of Carnival begins. In parts of Argentina the decorations for the Carnival are inspired as much by folk religion as by Christianity.

Magical, occult, and New Age spiritualism have found expression in Argentina, too.

Argentina has the largest Muslim minority in Latin America. The actual size of Argentina's Muslim community is estimated around 1.9 percent of the total population.

A cult has grown around the Dead Correa (La Difunta Correa), the unofficial patron saint of new beginnings. Legend has it that Deolinda Correa carried her baby across the desert in search of her soldier husband, but died of thirst; her baby was found alive, suckling at her breast.

There are little roadside shrines in Argentina where pilgrims bring bottles of water for Correa's soul. They believe that when the water evaporates, it has been drunk by Correa. Thousands of pilgrims visit the shrine near San Juan during Holy Week. To show gratitude for answered prayers, some pilgrims wear black mourning clothes, whereas others bring offerings, such as wedding dresses.

MIRACULOUS STATUES

Incredible tales about miraculous statues abound throughout Argentina. Here are the two of the most famous stories:

THE VIRGIN OF LUJÁN In 1630, before the town of Luján was founded, a man tried to drive an oxcart carrying a statue of the Virgin Mary over a plot of land. But no matter how many oxen were hitched to the cart, the statue would not move. The people decided that the Virgin Mary did not want her statue to leave its original spot, so they unloaded the statue and built a small chapel on the site. Later a large, richly decorated church was built to house the thousands of pilgrims who began coming to Luján every year to pray to the Virgin Mary. Luján is located about 44 miles (71 km) west of Buenos Aires.

Buenos Aires has the second-largest population of Jews in the Americas, second only to New York City.

THE CRUCIFIX OF SALTA In the 17th century a ship carrying a statue of the crucified Christ sank at sea on its way from Spain to the cathedral in

Salta Province in Argentina. Miraculously the statue floated to the coast of Peru, from where it was carried by a horse across the Andes to Salta, a distance of 1,600 miles (2,574 km).

There was a great celebration when the statue arrived safely. After the festivities the statue was packed and stored away in the cathedral's cellar for security.

A hundred years later a major earthquake shook Salta. When the people went to the cathedral to pray, they heard a voice saying that the quakes would not stop until the statue was put in its proper place in the cathedral. The statue was paraded around the city in a procession before being returned to the cathedral, and the quake stopped. Since then the crucifix of Salta has been paraded around the city every year to commemorate the event.

A stained-glass window of the Virgin of Luján in Merced Church, off San Martin Street in Ushuaia.

INTERNET LINKS

www.thearda.com/internationalData/countries/Country_11_2.asp /

This site from the the Association of Religion Data Archives provides statistics on the religious makeup of Argentina's population.

www.democracynow.org/2010/4/20/one

This site features a video about the importance of respecting Pachamama at the World People's Summit on Climate Change and the Rights of Mother Earth.

www.kwintessential.co.uk/articles/article/Argentina/Religion-in-Argentina/37

This site provides a concise, down-to-earth overview of the religions and their practices in Argentina.

A street kiosk in Buenos Aires carries all the latest local and international magazines.

JUST ABOUT EVERYBODY in Argentina speaks Spanish, the country's official language. Spanish is taught in all schools and is the only language used by the Argentine government.

SPANISH

The Spanish spoken in Argentina has local variations. The main Spanish dialect in Argentina is slightly different from the Spanish spoken in Spain, but people from both countries usually have no trouble understanding one another.

The influx of immigrants from Italy has influenced Argentine Spanish greatly, giving it an Italian accent and adding to it some Italian words.

9

The spoken languages of Argentina number at least 40, although Spanish is dominant.

A Spanish signboard at the Pozo del Las Animas. Spanish is Argentina's official language and is found on most official signboards in Argentina.

Argentina is the fifth-largest Spanish-speaking country after Mexico, the United States, Spain, and Colombia.

The influence of Italian is most noticeable around Buenos Aires and in the Pampas, where many Italians settled. Cocoliche was an Italian-Spanish pidgin that was spoken by Italian immigrants in Argentina (especially in Greater Buenos Aires) between 1880 and 1950. Sometimes "good-bye" becomes *chau* (chow), a variation of the Italian word *ciao*.

The mestizos in the north use dialects influenced by indigenous Indian languages, though generally these languages have less of an influence in Argentina than in many other South American countries due to the small number of indigenous Indians in Argentina. The descendants of immigrants from Mexico, Bolivia, Chile, and Paraguay speak in their own distinctive Spanish dialects.

OTHER VOICES

English is spoken throughout Argentina as a second language. Other languages, such as German, are still spoken by the descendants of immigrants in the larger towns and cities. Welsh is spoken by the descendants of Welsh immigrants in Patagonia.

Argentines love to chat over a drink, especially in cafés. European immigrants and indigenous peoples have lent great variety to the Spanish dialects used in Argentina.

Only a small number of the indigenous people of Argentina still speak Guaraní, Quechua, or other Indian languages. The names of these disappearing languages are quite musical: Aymará, Chiriguano, Chorotí, Mataco, Mocoví, Toba, Lule, Ranquel, Moleche, Tehuelche, and Ona. Scholars are making efforts to preserve and record the legends and oral traditions of Argentine Indians before their languages become extinct.

OF GANGSTERS AND TANGO SINGERS

Lunfardo (loon-FAR-doh) is a slang that is related to tango music, popular songs, and the theater. This dialect has influenced the Spanish spoken in Buenos Aires since around 1900. *Lunfardo* uses words borrowed from Italian, Portuguese, and many other languages.

Lunfardo began as a form of criminal slang. Words were borrowed, invented, and used in a way that could only be understood by those who used

Italian is the second most spoken language in Argentina.

the dialect. *Lunfardo* playfully changes the names of things. For instance, to speak of a person's head, the *lunfardo* speaker might choose words that mean "a bed of fleas," "thinker," "ball," or "the top of a building."

Soon poets and journalists discovered the colorful expressions of *lunfardo* and began to use them in their writing. Tango singers also began to use them in their songs. From 1916 poets wrote works in *lunfardo* with titles such as *Versos Rantifusos* (*Street Verses*) and *La Crencha Engrasada* (*Slicked-Down Hair*). The first tango to be sung had *lunfardo* lyrics and was called *Mi Noche Triste* (*My Night of Grief*). It was sung in 1917 by Carlos Gardel, the most famous of all tango singers. Gardel's fame and songs have endured long after his death in a plane crash in Colombia. Today Gardel's likeness is as iconic in Argentina as that of Eva Perón and Diego Maradona. His music is still played everywhere (and not just for tourists), and he is even referenced by the current generation of hip and cutting edge tango singers.

For a period of time, beginning in the 1940s, the government banned *lunfardo*. Nevertheless the dialect continued to enrich the spoken and written language of Buenos Aires. Over the years new words were added and old ones were dropped. In 1962 a group of scholars, artists, and radio people founded the Lunfardo Academy of Buenos Aires to preserve this distinctive language.

DID YOU KNOW . . . ?

Argentines tend to speak quickly, and they pronounce some consonants differently from the way Spaniards in Europe do. Some "s" sounds in Argentina are pronounced "th" in Spain. To a person used to the sounds of English, Castilian Spanish spoken in Spain sounds almost as if the speaker is lisping. In Argentina the "ll" sound is pronounced like a soft "j" or "sh." In other Spanish-speaking South American countries, such as Chile, "ll" sounds like a "y."

In written Spanish, question marks and exclamation marks appear not only at the end of a sentence but also upside down at the beginning of a sentence.

In Spanish the meaning of a word can change depending on which syllable is stressed. *Papá*, with the stress on the last syllable, means "father." *Papa*, with no stress on the final syllable, means "potato."

There is no A.M. or P.M. in Argentine Spanish. To say 8:00 A.M., a speaker must use words that translate as "eight in the morning." Airports and train and bus stations usually use a 24-hour clock. For example, when it is 3:00 P.M., these clocks read 15:00.

ARGENTINES LOVE TO READ

Argentina has a high literacy rate, and Argentines can read newspapers in Spanish and foreign languages. At least 150 daily newspapers are published. *La Prensa*, known for its excellent coverage of international news, and *La Nación* are two important dailies, each over 120 years old. Newspapers published in Buenos Aires are sold throughout most of the country. Major provincial cities also publish their own newspapers. The oldest in print is probably *La Capital*, founded in Rosario in 1867.

The degree of freedom enjoyed by the press has varied under different political regimes. *La Prensa* was seized by Juan Perón's officials in 1949 and was not returned to its owners until 1955. Publications have been banned because they were considered immoral or pro-communist by the government. In 1976 a period of book censorship began, and scholars were persecuted for their ideas. The present government allows artists and the media the freedom to express their views and criticisms.

Argentines of all ages enjoy reading newspapers as these men do at a park in San Salvador de Jujuy.

Since 2002, 60 new publishing companies have been founded, and Argentine society has a strong appreciation for books. More than a million people attended the book fair at Buenos Aires in 2008, which had 1,582 exhibitors.

Language **89**

The *Buenos Aires Herald*, founded in 1876, is the most prestigious English-language newspaper in South America. It is sold in all major cities in Argentina.

More than 4,000 publications come out every year in Argentina. The country's first magazine, *La Ilustración Argentina*, was printed in 1853. Picture magazines, such as *Gente* and *7 Días*, are very popular.

Argentine college students collaborating together on a school project.

RADIO AND TELEVISION AND INTERNET

Argentina has more than 100 radio stations and numerous television stations. Buenos Aires alone has four television stations—three are state owned and one is private. It is estimated that there is one radio for every 1.5 Argentines and one television set for every four Argentines. In comparison the averages for the United States are two radios per person and one television per 1.7 persons. Argentine viewers watch television programs imported from the United States and dubbed in Spanish. The number of Internet users in the country is estimated about 26 million, about half of all Argentines. The country has the second-highest number of Internet surfers on the continent, after Brazil.

EDUCATION AND LITERACY

Argentina has an impressive 97.2 percent literacy rate. Education is free from kindergarten to college. Most children attend seven grades of elementary school, even in rural areas where there are fewer schools.

The school year runs from March to December in most parts of the country. Lessons are taught in Spanish; English, French, and Italian are taught as second languages. Elementary school students may wear white coats over their own clothes. In many junior high schools, the students wear uniforms.

Although secondary education is not compulsory, there are free government schools in addition to private schools, in most big towns and cities. These offer five-year programs. Only a small percentage of students finish secondary school.

There are 95 public and private universities. The University of Buenos Aires is the largest, with more than 100,000 students. Founded in 1613 the University of Córdoba is the nation's oldest. Because many students work full-time, night courses are quite popular. The three most popular majors are architecture, political science, and medicine.

Children learning English at an Argentinean mission school.

Public schools largely owe their success to President Domingo Faustino Sarmiento (1811—88), who enlisted the advice of famous American educator Horace Mann to help set up the public school system. However, Argentina's school system is modeled closely after the French system. In the 1800s schools helped immigrant children adapt to Argentine society.

INTERNET LINKS

www.buenosairesherald.com/

This is the online site of the *Buenos Aires Herald*. It provides an insightful glimpse into Argentine society.

http://news.bbc.co.uk/2/hi/americas/country_profiles/1192478.stm#media

This site provides an overview of Argentina's media market.

www.ethnologue.com/show_country.asp?name=AR

This site offers an ethnologue showing the breakdown of languages in Argentina, from the extinct to the most widely spoken.

ARTS

The Museo de Arte Tigre art museum houses the works of many contemporary Argentine pieces.

10

I F THE HEART OF ARGENTINA is
its people, the soul of the country is
its artistic culture. Argentine artists
have excelled in a variety of fields,
including music, dance, literature,
architecture, painting, and sculpture.

Modern Argentine
culture has
been largely
influenced
by European
immigration,
although
there are also
elements of
Amerindian
and African
influences,
particularly in the
fields of music
and art.

PORTEÑO ART

Argentina's creative capital is the multicultural Buenos Aires region.
Porteño art takes its inspiration from the kaleidoscope of cultures
that have settled in the greater Buenos Aires area over the years.
Predominantly European in style, *porteño* art has nonetheless developed

Argentine gauchos playing along to traditional folk music.

A colorful wall mural in a subway station in Buenos Aires. Street art is very popular in Argentina, especially in the larger cities, where sculptures and murals are displayed in public for everyone to appreciate.

its own distinctive Argentine character. Today Buenos Aires is a thriving cultural center, boasting fine museums and art galleries, world-famous opera houses, and a number of theaters. The city's symphony orchestra, dance companies, and theater groups are established and well known abroad. Other large cities also house libraries, museums, theaters, and concert halls.

The power of Argentine artists has survived despite periods of great political repression. Some writers were forced to go into exile, whereas others courageously chose to stay and continue their work at home. The return of democracy to Argentina in the 1980s sparked a revival in the arts.

Unlike in most other Latin American countries, the indigenous arts in Argentina have had little influence on the overall development of the country's artistic culture. Still indigenous Argentines do produce woodcarvings, bolas, yerba mate sets, jewelry, and other handicrafts that exhibit a blend of Indian and Spanish traditions.

ART THROUGH ARGENTINE EYES

INDIGENOUS ART The oldest works of art found in Argentina are cave paintings and engravings. Small stone heads and a carving of a human foot with six toes have also been found.

The archaeological remains and pre-Columbian menhirs—tall stone columns—in Tafí del Valle in Tucumán Province are particularly striking. Tall-standing stones, some 10 feet (3 m) high, have been collected in Menhir Park. Scholars, however, cannot agree on their age or the meaning of their inscriptions.

The Diaguita, an indigenous group, created circles of engraved stones. Dozens of these stones remain in Tafí del Valle, a valley sacred to the Diaguita.

Prehistoric ceramics of the Condorhuasi culture are known by their strange shapes, with animal and human characteristics.

The Pachamama Inca museum, in Amaicha houses all the traditional Indian handicrafts. Although Argentina's indigenous civilizations did not reach the artistic height of the Incas in Peru, they did produce beautiful and artistic crafts.

COLONIAL AND POSTINDEPENDENCE ART   After the arrival of the Spanish and throughout colonial times, religious themes dominated the country's artistic scene. Manuel Belgrano founded the School of Geometry, Perspective and Drawing in Buenos Aires during the colonial period.

Prilidiano Pueyrredón and Cándido López dominated Argentina's 19th-century art scene. Carlos Morel and Fernando García Molina are painters who became famous in the 1830s. In more recent times Benito Quinquela Martín and Uruguayan-born Pedro Figari have depicted life in present-day Buenos Aires. Quinquela belongs to the La Boca group, a group of painters from the first two decades of the 20th century that were strongly influenced by Italian immigration and developed a distinctive style centered on labor and immigrant neighborhoods. A great portion of Pedro Figari's work focuses on the Afro-Uruguayan community, and the memories of his youth during the 19th century.

Lucio Fontana and Fernando Arranz are well known for their work in ceramics. The sculptures of Julio le Parc and Alicia Peñalba are widely known within and beyond Argentina. Photographer Pedro Luis Raota has won awards in at least 22 countries.

A typical artist's workshop in Argentina. This artist uses his oil paintings to explore the spirit of indigenous peoples and the lives of the gauchos. Among contemporary techniques, he uses objects and installations to confront them with ancestral masks, fabrics made of natural fibers, and ceramics.

Modern Argentine artists have reverted to creating works of art for the sake of their artistic value, rather than to make political criticism or social commentary. Some artists have blurred the distinction between photography, painting, and sculpture. The visual and dramatic arts are sometimes combined in performance pieces.

The works of Argentine artists can be admired in more than 100 art galleries in Buenos Aires as well as in the numerous galleries and museums found in the smaller cities.

GAUCHO ART

The gaucho has inspired Argentine literature, painting, and music. His rugged, courageous, and rustic way of life is seen as embodying the ideal lifestyle of an Argentine.

However, the gaucho was not always regarded as the romantic hero he is today. President Domingo Sarmiento (1868—74) attacked the legend of the proud, rebellious gaucho in *Civilization and Barbarism: Life of Juan Facundo Quiroga* (1845). Sarmiento felt that education, not rebellion, was the key to

JORGE LUIS BORGES (1899–1986)

Probably the most famous of Argentine writers, Jorge Luis Borges wrote essays, poetry, and short stories that inspired an entire generation of writers. Borges was admired for his brilliant use of language and his original thoughts about the meaning of life and other philosophical questions. His stories, which critics have compared to the stories of Edgar Allan Poe, convey a sense of mystery and fantasy.

Borges's international outlook on literature may have sprung from his family roots. His father was of Spanish, Portuguese, and English heritage, while his mother was of Argentine and Uruguayan heritage. Borges studied in Switzerland and published his first poem in Spain. He disapproved of Perón but took no active part in politics. In 1927 Borges began to lose his vision and was completely blind by the age of 56. With the help of assistants, books and writing remained the passion of his life. At age 68, he wed for the first time, but the marriage did not last. Shortly before his death, he married his 41-year-old assistant.

Among Borges's best-known books available in English are Ficciones (Fictions) *and* El Aleph *("aleph" is the first letter of the Hebrew alphabet). Borges won many literary honors, including Spain's most important literary award, the Cervantes Prize, in 1980. He was nominated for the Nobel Prize, but never won it.*

the country's future. *El Gaucho Martín Fierro* (1872), an epic poem by José Hernández, changed this view of the gaucho. Describing in vivid detail the difficult life of a gaucho, this poem is considered a literary masterpiece. As Argentina's "national poem," it is still read in schools. Hernández's portrait was sympathetic to the plight of the gauchos. He portrayed the people they often fought with—indigenous Indians, Afro-Argentines, the military, and the police—and depicted the forces that threatened the gaucho way of life.

Novelists influenced by Hernández include Benito Lynch and Ricardo Güiraldes. Güiraldes's *Don Segundo Sombra* (1926) imaginatively portrayed the decline of the gaucho. A group of young writers in the 1920s, known as the Martinfierristas, published a literary review called *Martín Fierro*. World-famous writer Jorge Luis Borges was a member of this group.

The father of Argentine national music, Alberto Williams, composed a piece called *Aires de la Pampa*, inspired by gaucho life in 1893.

Built originally as Cine Teatro Grand Splendid in 1919, the El Ateneo bookstore now occupies the interior of this historic building.

THE WRITTEN WORD

Many Argentine writers first came to the attention of the outside world when their works were published in the literary magazine *Sur*. The magazine was founded in 1931 by Victoria Ocampo, a rich, aristocratic writer. She also published short stories and poems by foreign writers in Spanish translation, introducing foreign literature to the Argentine public.

The most famous Argentine writers of the last century include Jorge Luis Borges, Leopoldo Lugones, Manuel Ugarte, Alfredo Palacios, Ernesto Sábato, Julio Cortázar, Manuel Puig, and Adolfo Bioy-Casares. Famous female writers include Alfonsina Storni, Silvina Ocampo, Norah Lange, Olga, Orozco, and Alejandra Pizarnik.

Bioy-Casares wrote a chronicle of porteño life called *Asleep in the Sun*, among other books. He also collaborated with Jorge Luis Borges on several books, published under a common pseudonym. Cortázar is known for his short stories and novels, such as *Rayuela*, and his works have been translated into many languages.

Celeste Goes Dancing is an engaging sample in English translation of stories written in the 1980s by 14 representative Argentine writers.

MUSEUMS AND SCIENTISTS

The National Museum of Fine Arts, opened in Buenos Aires in 1896, is becoming a showcase for the works of local artists. Today the museum houses works by modern Argentine and foreign artists as well as 400-year-old paintings illustrating Argentina's early history.

Other museums in Buenos Aires include the Museum of Spanish-American Art, with its valuable collection of colonial artifacts and silver pieces, and the Pharmacy Museum, where antiques from old pharmacies are on display. The José Hernández Museum specializes in the culture of the gauchos. The Malba in Buenos Aires (Museo de Arte Latinoamericano de Buenos Aires) was inaugurated in 2001. Its mission is to collect, conserve, study, and disseminate Latin American art, dating from the early 20th century to the present day. The city of Rosario has an excellent Museum of Modern Art. Founded in 1877 the Natural Science Museum in La Plata has a world-famous fossil collection. Many of the fossils were discovered by Florentino Ameghino (1854—1911), one of the world's first paleontologists, in the Pampas and in Patagonia.

Jacobo Timmerman, a newspaper editor, gained international recognition with his book *Prisoner Without a Name, Cell Without a Number* (1981). After being treated brutally by the military authorities, Timmerman accused them of attacking him not only because he had expressed dissent against the government but also because he was a Jew.

BENITO QUINQUELA MARTÍN AND LA BOCA

If an artist could change the look of a city, painter Benito Quinquela Martín (1890–1977) was the right person for the job. He first built a primary school for poor children of La Boca, formerly a slum area of Buenos Aires. When he handed the school to the city, it was on the condition that the school also house a museum of waterfront paintings. As a result La Boca became an art neighborhood, with Quinquela as one of its most famous artists.

Quinquela persuaded a number of restaurant owners in La Boca to paint their buildings in bright colors. Owners of run-down homes in the neighborhood followed suit, painting them in vivid reds, yellows, and blues. Quinquela also established an open-air market to promote the work of local artists.

The riverfront section of La Boca remains a favorite gathering spot for artists and poets. Tourists enjoy the view of the colorful buildings. Nostalgic music pouring out of clubs brings visitors back in time to when the tango was first played in the dance halls of La Boca.

MUSIC AND DANCE

Composers in Argentina have been influenced by both European and gaucho music. In the 17th century Jesuit missionaries taught music to the indigenous Indians as a form of evangelism. Amancio Alcorta (1805–62) is considered to be Argentina's first local-born composer. His main works include waltzes, polkas, and other kinds of dance music. Born to a wealthy family in Santiago del Estero, Alcorta served in Argentina's senate.

Italian immigrants gave Argentina a taste for opera. Today opera is second only to the tango in popularity. More than 70 Argentine operas have been produced at home and abroad. Alberto Ginastera's opera *Bomarzo* is remembered for its violent theme and its dramatic impact on audiences.

Folk dancing thrives in provinces such as Salta. Dance styles resemble Incan, Spanish, gaucho, and other Latin American forms of dancing.

ARGENTINA'S TANGO The passionate tango is Argentina's most famous cultural contribution to the world. As a dance, the tango is performed by a couple holding each other tightly and gliding together in long, elegant steps, occasionally pausing in dramatic poses. The accompanying lyrics are often a melancholic musing on lost love.

A pair of tango dancers strikes a dramatic pose.

Neo-tango incorporates jazz and classical influences into a more experimental style. "Electrotango" is blended acoustic tango and electronic music.

The tango appeared in the late 1800s and gained worldwide popularity in the early 1900s. Some scholars trace its roots to gypsy music in Spain, whereas others say it developed from the *milonga* (mee-LOHN-gah)—an earlier dance popular in Argentina—and other dances such as the polka. Tango music is generally played by guitar, violin, flute, piano, and especially *bandoneón* (bahn-doh-NYOHN), an instrument similar to the accordion. People who dance the tango are called "tango interpreters."

Originating in the working class, the tango was at first considered vulgar by the upper class. In the 1920s the pope declared that dancing the tango was not a sin. Its popularity then spread to the upper classes in Buenos Aires and to other countries around the world. *Milonga* is a term for a place or an event where tango is danced. People who frequently go to *milongas* are sometimes

The Teatro Colón is one of the world's largest and most elegant opera houses. Built between 1887 and 1908, it is considered the finest concert hall in Latin America where many famous tango artists had their music recorded.

Argentina is a major producer of motion pictures, and the local film industry produces around 80 full-length titles annually.

called *milongueros*. Due to the strict assembly ban imposed by the military government, *milongas* almost disappeared from Buenos Aires in the 1960s and 1970s. Nevertheless, since the beginning of the 1990s, the tango culture in Buenos Aires has undergone dynamic range of development, and today one can choose from between 15 and 30 different *milongas* every day.

Cuarteto (quartet) is a musical genre that found its roots in Córdoba, Argentina. In the 1970s *cuarteto* became one of the cornerstones of Córdoba's cultural identity. The roots of the *cuarteto* ensemble are in Italian and Spanish dance ensembles. The name was coined because the early dance-hall numbers were invariably four-piece bands (violin-piano-accordion-bass). *Cuarteto* was one of the genres that gave birth to the Buenos Aires *tropical* scene, which was renamed *bailanta* in the 1990s following the usage of Corrientes Province.

FILM

Argentina's movie industry developed after World War I. Buenos Aires and Mexico City became Latin America's main filmmaking capitals from the 1930s to the 1950s.

Argentine movies have won awards in film festivals around the world. In the United States *The Official Story* won an Oscar for Best Foreign Film in 1985. Actress Norma Aleandro was nominated for Best Actress in that film. She portrayed a woman who discovers that her adopted daughter is the child of one of the "disappeared." *Kiss of the Spider Woman*, a film based on Argentine Manuel Puig's novel, also depicted the government's persecution of the people. Actor William Hurt won the Academy Award for Best Actor in that film in 1986. *The Secret in Their Eyes* (*El secreto de sus ojos*) is the last Argentine movie to win the Academy Award for best foreign movie (2010). Although the local filmmaking industry is thriving, movies imported from the United States and Europe are still the most popular among Argentines.

ARCHITECTURE

Colonial buildings are well preserved in northern Argentina, where the first Spanish settlers built the country's oldest towns. Córdoba's cathedral, completed in 1784, is a beautiful example of colonial architecture. Following Spanish practice, the cathedral faces a plaza, or open square. In the countryside many lavish estates were built in the colonial style.

The buildings in Buenos Aires display Spanish and Italian influences, but visitors feel the city resembles Paris the most. Wide boulevards, apartment buildings with charming balconies, and large government buildings dating from the 1800s remind many visitors of the French capital. Numerous parks and gardens, many exhibiting marble statues and fountains, add to the beauty of the city.

César Pelli's futurist creation and contribution to the skyline of Buenos Aires is the Edificio República. Futurist architecture is characterized by long horizontal lines suggesting speed, motion, and urgency.

INTERNET LINKS

www.en.argentina.ar/_en/culture/C180-literature-with-history.php

This site discusses how Argentina's history influences its literature. It includes videos of interviews with a writer, a documentary on Argentine comics, and a street parade in Buenos Aires.

www.totango.net/sergio.html

This site provides a history of the evolution of Argentine tango.

www.tangosouth.co.uk/about-tango/but-what-is-argentine-tango/

This site contains videos of a classic Argentine tango.

LEISURE

Like the tourists, many local Argentines also enjoy swimming and sunbathing at the Playa Varese resort in the city of Mar del Plata.

11

THE NAME *BUENOS AIRES*, or "Good Winds," comes from the early Spaniards' gratitude to the Virgin of the Good Winds, a Catholic saint, for their safe arrival in this land. Argentines still enjoy good winds and fresh air near beautiful lakes and rivers, the Atlantic Ocean, and the Andes Mountains.

These places boast ideal conditions for camping, hunting, fishing, hiking, mountain climbing, skiing, sailing, windsurfing, and cycling. Argentines also take vacations in resort areas such as Bariloche.

The practice of sports in Argentina is varied due to the country's multicultural population. Argentina's mostly mild climate favors outdoor activities throughout the year.

Families enjoy relaxing walks together at the Palermo Park in Buenos Aires.

Men playing soccer in Cafayete, their field surrounded by towering mountains. Many Argentine boys dream of becoming soccer stars.

Team sports attract many Argentines, both players and spectators. Besides soccer, the national sport, other sports such as basketball, cricket, polo, and rugby are extremely popular in Argentina. Fans heartily cheer their favorite teams and players during playoffs and final matches. The Argentines have been known to celebrate a favorite team's victory with festivities that last for days.

Following the gaucho tradition, the Argentines in the Pampas like rugged contests on horseback. Unlike in many other Spanish-speaking countries, however, bullfighting is not popular in Argentina.

A PASSION FOR SOCCER

The most popular sport in Argentina is soccer, or *fútbol* (FOOT-bohl) in Spanish. The English brought this game to Argentina in the 19th century.

Children grow up playing soccer at school, in the street, or in any open space. Competition to be selected for a prestigious team is fierce. Boys who manage to become professional soccer players can expect to earn big salaries. Star players often become national heroes.

In Buenos Aires a traditional rivalry exists between the Boca Juniors team from the Italian neighborhood of La Boca and the River Plate team from the Belgrano neighborhood of Buenos Aires. Three-quarters of the nation's soccer fans support one of these two teams.

Among the national teams, a passionate rivalry exists between Argentina and Brazil. In the past more than 100,000 fans have turned out to watch individual games between the two countries.

Argentina has won successive Olympic gold medals in soccer in 2004 and 2008. It has also won the FIFA Club World Cup nine times.

SMALL BUT MIGHTY

A few years ago Argentina's Diego Armando Maradona was considered the best soccer player in the world. His fiery personality, tremendous athletic skill, and superb performances have made him the subject of many stories. The 5-foot, 5-inch (1.65-m) star from the poor Villa Fiorito slum in Buenos Aires has earned a variety of nicknames, from "golden boy" and "king of soccer" to "Mr. Disagreeable." Maradona sported the number 10 on his jersey, the number traditionally given to a team's best scorer. Soccer's greatest star, Pelé, also wore number 10. Much like Pelé's story, Maradona's life is also a rags-to-riches story.

Maradona has played for teams on both sides of the Atlantic. He played for Italy's Napoli club and led Argentina's team in three World Cups, including their most recent win in 1986. Since the early 1990s Maradona has had a rocky relationship with drug abuse. He was twice suspended from playing for using illegal drugs and finally retired from the field in 1997. In 1998 he traveled with the Argentine national team to comment on the World Cup and was known to be negotiating to coach the 2002 team.

It was confirmed in October 2008 that Maradona would be the head coach of the Argentine football team. After winning his first three matches in charge of the national team, he oversaw a 6—1 loss to Bolivia, equaling the team's worst-ever margin of defeat. With two matches remaining in the qualification tournament for the 2010 World Cup, Argentina was in fifth place and faced the possibility of failing to qualify, but victory in the last two matches secured qualification for the finals.

After Argentina's qualification for the 2010 World Cup, Maradona used abusive language at the live postgame press conference. FIFA responded with a two-month ban on all soccer activity, which expired on January 15, 2010, and a hefty fine, with a warning as to his future conduct. After the 2010 World Cup, his contract was not renewed.

Lionel Andrés "Leo" Messi is an Argentine soccer player who currently plays for Football Club Barcelona and the Argentina national team as a forward or winger. He also holds Spanish citizenship, which makes him eligible as an EU player. Considered one of the best soccer players of his generation and frequently cited as the world's best contemporary player, Messi received several Ballons d'Or and FIFA World Player of the Year nominations by the age of 21 and he won both by the age of 22. He also won the 2010 FIFA Ballon d'Or at the age of 23. His playing style and ability have drawn comparisons to Diego Maradona, who himself declared Messi his "successor."

Messi began playing football at a young age and his potential was quickly identified by Barcelona. He left Rosario-based Newell's Old Boys youth team in 2000 and moved with his family to Europe, as Barcelona offered treatment for his growth hormone deficiency. Making his debut in the 2004—05 season,

he broke his team's record for the youngest soccer player to score a league goal. His breakthrough season was in the 2006—07 season; he became a first team regular, scoring a hat-trick in El Clásico and finishing with 14 goals in 26 league games. Perhaps his most successful season was the 2008—09 season, in which Messi scored 38 goals to play an integral part in a treble-winning campaign. In the following 2009—10 campaign, Messi scored 47 goals in all competitions, equaling Ronaldo's record total for Barcelona.

Messi was the top scorer of the 2005 FIFA World Youth Championship with six goals, including two in the final game. Shortly thereafter he became an established member of Argentina's senior international team. In 2006 he became the youngest Argentine to play in the FIFA World Cup and he won a runners-up medal at the Copa América tournament the following year. In 2008 in Beijing, he won his first international honor, an Olympic gold medal, with the Argentina Olympic football team.

Some of Argentina's best soccer players are recruited to play for famous foreign clubs, particularly in Europe. Brazil and Mexico also hire Argentine players. However, these soccer stars often return home to play for Argentina's national team in the World Cup games.

Argentina's long list of honors in its soccer history includes winning the Junior World Championship in 1979 and the World Cup in 1978 and 1986. In the 1990 World Cup championship, after defeating Brazil and later their host country Italy, Argentina lost to West Germany in the final. Nevertheless Sergio Goycochea, the substitute goalkeeper who stepped in during the final matches, became a national hero due to his superb and inspirational performance on the field.

Enthusiastic fans gather to support their favorite team in the River Plate soccer stadium in Buenos Aires.

BRITISH HORSEBACK

The game of polo, played on specially bred ponies, was brought to Argentina by British immigrants. Drawing on their gaucho tradition of great horsemanship, Argentines quickly took to the game.

In Buenos Aires crowds of 20,000 people routinely turn out to cheer for their favorite players. Gonzalo Pieres, a national polo hero, is also ranked as one of the world's best.

Polo players begin their training as children, swinging little mallets from bicycles. They then join polo leagues to compete against other teams. Argentina's best polo players usually come from families that own large farms. Players can practice year-round on the farm. Family teams of fathers, sons, uncles, and cousins are common. Prized for their speed and ability to work with their riders, Argentine polo ponies are some of the most expensive of their type in the world.

Polo players in team action at Campo de Polo. Like soccer, polo was introduced into Argentina by British immigrants in the 1800s.

The three most important polo tournaments in the world, the Argentine Open, the Hurlingham Open, and the Tortugas Open, are held in Argentina. Argentina has been the uninterrupted world champion since 1949 and is today the source of most of the world's top 10 players of polo.

Show-jumping is another sport that has given local riders international recognition. The National Polo Fields and the Argentine Horsetrack are located in the suburb of Palermo. As Argentines love to attend horse races, a new race track has been built in the Buenos Aires suburb of San Isidro.

GAUCHO HORSEBACK

The horseback game of *pato* (PAH-toh) originated with the gauchos. *Pato* was originally played using a live duck (*pato* is Spanish for "duck"). The duck was placed in a sack with its head sticking out. Two teams would race over a 3-mile-long (4.8-km-long) field fighting over the sack. Because the games often ended in violent, bloody fights, the local government banned *pato* in 1822. The game was legalized again under President Juan Manuel de Rosas. Today a six-handled, inflated leather bag has replaced the duck. To score points, players must land the bag in a netted iron hoop 3 feet (91 cm) in diameter at the opponent's end of the playing field. *Pato* has traditionally been a working-class game, but its popularity has spread to other social groups. As in polo, *pato* horses are valued for their speed, strength, endurance, and ability to work with their riders.

In the game of *sortija* (sor-TEE-ha), a horseman gallops at full speed and tries to lance a small ring, or *sortija*, hanging from a bar. Much skill is needed, since the ring may be as tiny as a wedding ring.

SCALING THE HEIGHTS

Mountain climbers from around the world come to Argentina to attempt to reach the tops of the Andes peaks. Mendoza, about 800 miles (1,290 km) west of Buenos Aires, is Argentina's most popular spot for mountain climbing. Mount Aconcagua, the highest peak in the Western Hemisphere, poses a challenge to expert climbers. Matias Zurbriggen from Switzerland was the first to reach the summit of Mount Aconcagua in 1897. There are 10 recognized routes up the mountain, but most climbers use the northern route.

Teams from Germany, Italy, Switzerland, and the United States have attempted to climb Mount Aconcagua. Over the years the peak has claimed many lives; climbers who die on the mountain are usually buried in a small cemetery at its foot.

Hang-gliding is also popular in Argentina. The sport is sponsored by the nation's air force. International competitions are held in the hills near Córdoba, an area famous for challenging wind drafts.

Adventurous climbers scaling the Perito Moreno glacier of Los Glaciares National Park in Patagonia.

SPORTS HEROES

Argentina has produced many sports heroes. Although Juan Fangio won the world championship Grand Prix races five times, other Argentines such as Carlos Alberto Reutemann—a famous Grand Prix driver—and Ricardo Zunino have quickly followed in his tracks.

The most famous Argentine boxer is probably Luis Angel Firpo, who fought in the 1920s. He was called "the wild bull of the Pampas" and has been honored with a statue in Buenos Aires. He knocked world heavyweight champion Jack Dempsey out of the ring in 1923, but lost the match. Other Argentine boxers have been world champions in various categories. Carlos Monzón held the middleweight title from 1970 to 1977.

RACING LEGEND JUAN FANGIO

Juan Manuel Fangio (1911—95) was born in poverty but acquired international fame and wealth through competitive sports.

In the 1950s racing star Fangio won the Grand Prix championship five times. The lives of racing drivers then were glamorous but risky. Drivers wore neither hard helmets nor flame-proof clothing. Thirty drivers—all of them Fangio's friends—died in flaming wrecks at the prime of their careers in that decade alone. Although not a rarity today fatal race track accidents have become less common than in the past. This is due in no small part to technological advances in automobile safety features, such as better brakes and wider tires.

In his autobiography Fangio devoted an entire chapter to the topic of luck. Fangio's belief was that "no one dies before a day that is marked." He also said that "whenever someone was killed, I thought to myself, surely he committed an error." Due to such remarks, he was accused of being cold-blooded. In fact old newsreels show him driving skillfully past burning wrecks, as they rolled into screaming spectators. Fangio trusted his skills, his mechanics, and his cars. He had two accidents in which his co-driver died. Fangio later blamed those crashes on his lack of sleep.

Fangio grew up in a poor family and, as a child, worked long hours in a garage. Perhaps it was there that he gained his legendary ability to communicate with the engines and tires of his cars. During his first race, in 1929, he drove a Ford taxi but later won races driving Alfa Romeos, Mercedes-Benzes, Ferraris, and Maseratis. After his retirement, at the top of his career, Fangio became president of Mercedes-Benz in South America. He founded a museum in his hometown of Balcarce, where 500 of his trophies and 50 of his racing and classic cars are on display.

Argentina's international tennis stars include Guillermo Vilas, José Luis Clerc, Ivanna Madruga, and Gabriela Sabatini. In 1983, at the age of 13, Sabatini became the youngest player to win the Orange Bowl trophy for players under 18 years of age.

Rugby star Hugo Porta, who made his debut in 1971, is considered one of the greatest players of all time. He later served as Argentina's ambassador to South Africa and as the country's sports secretary.

Argentina has also produced a number of outstanding swimmers. In 1962, at the age of 17, Luis Alberto Nicolao broke the world record in the 100-meter butterfly style. More recently José Meolans won second place in the 100-meter swimming competition at the Goodwill Games held in Australia.

Fishing championships are held in Bariloche each year. A record 36-pound (16-kg) trout was caught in that region. Competitions are also held each year in Paso de la Patria, a town on the Paraná River in the northeast. People compete to catch the largest golden dorado, a fighting fish that can weigh up to 60 pounds (27 kg).

In 1978 Argentina won the world championship ice hockey title.

By the time he retired from racing in 1959, Juan Fangio had won 16 world championship Grand Prix races, including four consecutive German title races.

INTERNET LINKS

www.lionelmessi.com/

This site will tell you everything you could want to know about Lionel Messi.

www.argentina.ar/_en/sports/C269-polo-in-argentina.php?idioma_sel=en

This site provides a brief overview of polo in Argentina, including videos.

www.argentinesoccer.com

This site contains information about soccer in Argentina, with daily updates.

FESTIVALS

Dancers accompany this float at the Gualeguaychu Carnival in Entre Rios. Carnival celebrations in Argentina usually begin in the early evening and last until the early hours of the morning.

12

WHEN ARGENTINA COMES ALIVE with festivals, or fiestas, colorful parades brighten the landscape from one end of the country to the other. Argentines in different parts of the country express their artistic, musical, and culinary creativity through festivals that reflect indigenous and Christian traditions.

ARGENTINE FESTIVALS

Some festivals commemorate historical events. For example each city celebrates the anniversary of its founding. In other festivals people celebrate the legends and traditions of the many cultures that have enriched Argentina's history.

Young women performing in celebration of Independence Day in Chilecito.

Throughout the year in Argentina national holidays are celebrated with Argentine traditions that have been passed down from generation to generation and defined region by region.

Men dressed in traditional gaucho fashion making their way to the Fiesta Gaucha held in San Antonio de Areco. This exciting annual gaucho festival is held over the first ten days of November.

Argentine festivals and holidays may involve religious pilgrimages, feasts, parades, dancing, and sometimes gaucho horseback competitions. Most of the competitors in horseback events are descendants of the traditional gauchos. They use old costumes and saddles for the contest. The Gaucho Festival of San Antonio de Areco, 80 miles (128 km) north of Buenos Aires, takes place from November 10 to November 17.

The traditions of immigrant communities form the basis for some Argentine festivals. The Welsh singing festival takes place in October in Trevelin, a Patagonian mountain town near Esquel. A gathering of Welsh musicians and poets also takes place each year at Gaiman in Patagonia.

WINE, MATE, WHEAT, AND PONCHOS

Some Argentine festivals celebrate the chief agricultural products of a region. In Mendoza, the winemaking area along the Andes, the Vendimia Festival is celebrated in March to mark the grape harvest. Honoring more than 1,500 wine producers from the region, it is one of the most impressive festivals in Latin America. The vines are blessed in a special ceremony, fountains of red wine are free for the crowd to taste, a festival queen is chosen, and a magnificent parade is held. The people of Mendoza also celebrate their history. At the end of February, before the wine festival begins, they commemorate General San Martín's crossing of the Andes.

In Posadas, the capital of the province of Misiones, the people hold an annual festival to celebrate the harvest of mate, a holly brewed to make yerba mate, the national drink. Ornately decorated coaches carrying young ladies from every district of the province parade through the streets of Posadas, and one of the girls is chosen as the year's mate queen.

The most important wheat festival in Argentina takes place in Leones in the province of Córdoba. A wheat queen is chosen at the commercial and industrial fair, and a number of folkloric events are celebrated. People in the central farming province of La Pampa also celebrate harvest festivals.

The Fiesta del Poncho in Catamarca features the local production of handwoven ponchos. The fleece for these garments comes from three animals that live high in the Andes Mountains—the alpaca, the llama, and the vicuña. The people of Catamarca proudly display their ponchos as a symbol of a continuing ancient tradition. For the gauchos, ponchos were an indispensable piece of clothing that protected them from the cold and strong winds of the Pampas.

Although less lavish than its Brazilian neighbors' festival, the Argentine Carnival gives the locals a day to dress up and enjoy the festivities.

CARNIVAL

Carnival is a festivity often celebrated in Catholic countries around the world. Mardi Gras in the United States is a celebration that originated in Carnival festivities. The celebration of Carnival in Argentina is particularly lavish in the northern part of the country. Business comes to a halt as Argentines dressed in outrageous costumes dance in the streets.

Carnival festivities begin on the weekend before Ash Wednesday, which usually falls in February. In the northeast the celebrations are mixed with Indian traditions. In Tilcara floral arrangements representing the Stations of the Cross are hung along the streets, and processions come down the mountains on Ash Wednesday.

Carnival in Argentina is not celebrated with the same abandon as it is in Brazil. Visitors, however, may find that many Argentines are often attending parties and that business is interrupted during Carnival. Typical ways of celebrating include holding drinking parties until the early hours of the morning and drenching one another with water balloons. Hotels and clubs in major cities hold parties during Carnival.

REGIONAL FESTIVALS

A colorful regional festival takes place somewhere in Argentina almost every month of the year. In Puerto Madryn an underwater fishing festival kicks off the New Year. In Rosario del Tala the Tango Festival runs through the first half of January. The last half of January is devoted to a two-week National Folklore Festival in Cosquín in the province of Córdoba. An artisan fair is held in Cosquín at almost the same time.

On February 2 processions on horseback at Humahuaca near Jujuy bring pilgrims to the Candelaria Virgin. Fireworks, traditional foods, and religious music add to the celebrations. Northern Argentines meet with southern Bolivians during Easter week to trade handicrafts and other goods. They also

Folkloristic dancers perform at the International Music Day festival in Salta.

meet on the last two Sundays of October at the Manca Fiesta, or Festival of the Pot, where trading takes place.

Salta Week, starting on June 14, marks the anniversary of a local battle. While San Martín was fighting the Spanish, Salta's town hero, General Martín Miguel de Güemes, led a band of gauchos against the Spanish in the Gaucho War. This festival includes fireworks, colorful floats, singing, and dancing. Salta is also noted for its Christmas performances, tableaux, and caroling, which continue for weeks.

Corrientes, which has a particularly lively Carnival celebration, marks its founding on May 3 with a religious and popular arts festival.

On June 24 Saint John's Day is celebrated in several towns. In Formosa the faithful walk barefoot over a bed of hot coals. Every year on July 25 processions in Salta, Jujuy, and Mendoza honor Saint James. Saint Anne is honored a day later in Tilcara, near Jujuy.

Also in July, Argentines gather at the annual Livestock Exhibition at the Argentine Rural Society in Buenos Aires. Cattle, horses, sheep, and pigs are judged for prizes and sold at auctions.

The small village of Villa General Belgrano hosts an Alpine Chocolate Festival every winter and an authentic Oktoberfest, or German beer festival.

Thousands of Catholic believers make a pilgrimage several times a year to celebrate the Fiesta of Our Lady of Luján, the patron saint of Argentina. Many make the journey from their homes to Luján on foot. Early in December old coaches from a colonial museum in Luján parade around town as part of the festivities.

MUSICAL CELEBRATIONS

The northwest of Argentina is the region with the oldest history of Spanish settlement. At the same time, it remains the heart of indigenous Indian culture. The region's history has contributed to unique musical celebrations that blend both Indian and Spanish traditions.

Traditional Indian customs are preserved through colorful celebrations, such as the *misachicos* (mee-sah-CHEE-kos), the carnival of Jujuy, and other religious festivals.

PUBLIC HOLIDAYS

Official public holidays include both religious and historical celebrations.

- *January 1—New Year's Day*
- *January 6—Epiphany*
- *March/April—Maundy Thursday, Good Friday, and Easter Sunday*
- *March 24—This was declared the National Day of Memory for Truth and Justice in remembrance of the state of siege of 1976.*
- *May 1—Labor Day*
- *May 25—Anniversary of the Revolution of 1810*
- *June 10—Malvinas Day, commemorating the Falklands War*
- *June 20—Flag Day*
- *July 9—Independence Day*
- *August 17—Anniversary of the death of General José de San Martín, the liberator of Argentina*
- *October 12—Columbus Day*
- *December 8—Catholic feast of the Immaculate Conception*
- *December 25—Christmas*

On these occasions musicians come down from the mountains to crowd the narrow, steep streets of the colonial villages. They bring with them *erkes* (EHR-kes), long trumpets that make a loud, distinctive sound that is audible from a distance; *charangos* (chah-RAHN-gos), small guitars made from the carcasses of local armadillos; and typical bass drums.

The joyful music of indigenous Argentines comes to life in these celebrations. *Carnavalitos* (kahr-nah-vah-LEE-tohs), *bagualas* (bah-goo-AH-lahs), *zambas* (SAHM-bahs), *cuecas* (koo-EH-kahs), and *chacareras* (chah-kah-RAY-rahs) are some local musical tunes. They are sometimes played with indigenous instruments such as *erkes*, *charangos*, bass drums, *bombos* (BOHM-bohs), *sikus* (SEE-koos), and *quenas* (KAY-nahs); other times, they are also played with European instruments, such as guitars, violins, and large accordions.

TWO INDEPENDENCE DAYS

The longstanding rivalry between the people of Buenos Aires and the people living in the provinces has resulted in Argentines celebrating two independence days.

May 25 marks the date when the people of Buenos Aires declared independence from Spain. The people of the provinces celebrate the holiday on July 9, when deputies of the interior Congress of Tucumán declared the United Provinces free. Today people in the capital and countryside celebrate both holidays.

During the May 25 celebrations, a lavish parade is held. The Plaza de Mayo is filled with army officers in riding boots, naval officers in 19th-century frock coats and spats, and soldiers massed in battle gear and black berets, in a re-enactment of the struggle for nationhood. As the proud symbol of Argentina, the regal gauchos ride on horseback, their red cloaks flowing in the wind.

Buenos Aires celebrates art with a Contemporary Dance Festival, an International Independent Film Festival, an International Jazz Festival, and an International Theater Festival, all of which take place at different times of the year.

INTERNET LINKS

www.2camels.com/festivals/argentina.php

Get to know the different festivals in Argentina, with links provided to each festival's website.

www.the-allure-of-argentina.com/argentinatraditions.html

This site gives an overview of Argentine traditions, festivals, observances, and celebrations, surrounding the national and main religious holidays.

www.carnavalescorrentinos.com/videos.php

The Carnival in Corrientes 2010—typical of the flamboyant Argentine Carnival.

FOOD

A street *asado* (Argentine barbecue) vendor selling steak and sausage sandwiches at a market in Mataderos.

AN ARGENTINE SAYING GOES that every Argentine is an expert at barbecuing, and no wonder, since beef is by far the most popular food, and some Argentines eat it three times a day.

Traditionally meat was spit-roasted in the courtyard of the home or in the fields. It was often pierced through a cross-shaped spit, one end of which was driven into the ground at an angle to keep the roast over the flames. At other times it was cooked on a grill over hot coals.

Today the average Argentine consumes 149 pounds (67.7 kg) of beef per year. Writers have attributed the overwhelming popularity of beef to a belief that eating it gives people the animal's vitality and that people must eat plenty of it to be strong. Perhaps the real reason why so much beef is consumed is that it is plentiful and cheap. Many people consider Argentine beef the best in the world, tender enough to be cut with just a fork.

Meat is so popular in Argentina that whole animals are barbecued over an open fire.

A typical meal consists of grilled beef with French fries, salad, and red wine. In restaurants beef is served in hearty portions. Some restaurants place a small stove at each table and barbecue the meats right in front of their customers. The meat is usually seasoned before it reaches the table.

It is not unusual for someone in the office to take a trip to the butcher's a little before lunchtime to buy some fresh meat to be roasted or grilled for his or her colleagues to eat for lunch. Argentines are slowly absorbing the news that eating less red meat may lower cholesterol levels and improve health. Still, grilled beef remains the favorite food among Argentines.

ARGENTINE MEALS

Aside from the predictable main course, side dishes can also have an Argentine flair. *Matambre* (mah-TAHM-breh), meaning "hunger killer," is an appetizer of baked marinated flank steak stuffed with spinach, hearts of palm, and ham or hard-boiled eggs. It can be eaten hot or cold. Another popular local dish is *bife a caballo,* a steak served with fried egg.

A café owner stands proudly before the assorted pastries and baked goods on the counter.

Lettuce and tomato salads are tossed with oil—often olive oil—and vinegar or lemon juice. The creamy and cheesy salad dressings common in the United States are rare in Argentina.

Desserts include fresh fruit and cheese and the much-loved *dulce de leche*—milk simmered with sugar until it thickens to a gooey, caramel consistency. This sweet concoction is used as a filling in other desserts.

Alfajores con dulce de leche is a pastry with two layers of dough and a filling, coated with powdered sugar. Each region of the country has its own style. For chocolate lovers, chocolate versions are plentiful and delicious. *Dulce de leche* is also spread on breakfast toast, eaten by the spoonful, served along with ice cream, and used in cakes and meringues. Sometimes it is eaten with cheese to cut its sweetness.

Rice pudding and *almendrado* (ahl-mehn-DRAH-doh), ice cream rolled in crushed almonds, also satisfy the Argentine sweet tooth. Italian-style ice creams abound throughout Argentina.

A typical meal consists of grilled beef, salad, and red wine.

INDIGENOUS FOOD

One of the few truly indigenous dishes in Argentina is *locro* (LAW-kroh), a thick corn stew. *Locro* contains beef, beans, potatoes, peppers, onions, and ingredients typical of the Andes.

The indigenous Indian influence on food is most noticeable in the north. In the northeast, near the famous Iguazú Falls, typical dishes created by the Guaraní include *chipa* (CHEE-pah), a small, hard biscuit made of manioc, eggs, and cheese.

Sopa paraguaya (SOH-pah pah-rah-WAH-yah) is a pie made of corn, cheese, and eggs. *Reviro* (reh-VEE-roh) is a breakfast dish made of milk, flour, eggs, and cheese.

In the northwest certain dishes reflect mestizo heritage. *Huminta en chala* (oo-MEEN-tah ehn CHAH-lah) is a mildly spicy cornmeal tamale cooked in corn husks.

INTERNATIONAL INFLUENCE

The food of Argentina is really a blend of Italian, Jewish, Spanish, Polish, and German foods. Only indigenous Indian dishes originated in Argentina. Contemporary Argentine cuisine reflects the different ethnic groups that immigrated and settled in the country.

The gauchos contributed the *asado* (ah-SAH-doh), beef roasted over an open wood or coal fire. *Bife a caballo* (BEE-feh ah kah-VAH-zhoh), or "beef on horseback," is a steak topped with fried eggs; *carbonada* (kar-boh-NAH-dah) is a stew made with beef, corn, squash, and peaches and baked in a pumpkin shell; *churrasco* (choor-RAHS-koh) is grilled steak; chorizos are spicy sausages; and *morcillas* (mohr-SEE-zhas) are blood sausages popular in German and Polish cooking.

At the *parrillada* (par-ree-ZHAH-da), a grill house that cooks meat over charcoal fires, one can order a *parrillada mixta*, or mixed grill. Some Argentines enjoy grilling an assortment of sausages, short ribs, and organ meats, such as kidneys, liver, and sweetbreads, and even cow's udders.

Empanadas served with beer. Such snacks are usually enjoyed in the afternoon or as a quick meal.

From Italy comes the *milanesa* (mee-lah-NEH-sah), thinly sliced beef coated with beaten egg and bread crumbs, then deep fried. Spanish cooking inspired *puchero de gallina* (poo-CHEH-roh day gah-ZHEE-nah), a chicken stew made with corn, sausages, potatoes, and squash. Children like *ñoquis* (NYOH-kees), potato dumplings served with meat and tomato sauce. Argentine empanadas derive from Great Britain's Cornish pastries. They are fried or baked crescent-shaped pastries, stuffed with chopped meats, cheese, creamed corn, fish, or seafood. Chopped hardboiled eggs, olives, and onions are sometimes used to flavor the filling.

FINDING FOOD

Eating out is a favorite activity in Argentina. There are many types of restaurants and shops that cater to the fussiest of diners. The great majority of restaurants feature beef. Some can seat hundreds of people and are open 24 hours a day. People may linger for hours over a three-course meal, and some restaurants hire orchestras to entertain diners.

Sidewalk cafés line the wide boulevards of Buenos Aires. Argentines take advantage of a moderate climate to enjoy English tea in the afternoon at outdoor tables.

The names of food shops sound like poetry—*pizzerías* (pee-tseh-REE-ahs); *cafeterías* (kah-feh-teh-REE-ahs); *heladerías* (eh-lah-deh-REE-ahs), which serve ice cream; and *confiterías* (kohn-fee-teh-REE-ahs), which serve cakes, sandwiches, empanadas, and simple meals. Because most restaurants offer the same menu at both lunch and dinner, the *confitería* is the place to go for a light noon meal. *Porteños* eat a light breakfast, a large lunch between noon and 3:00 P.M., late afternoon tea, and a huge late dinner between 10:00 P.M. and midnight. Restaurants usually stay open until 2:00 A.M. Also, Argentines enjoy spending time at the coffee houses. Cafés are an intrinsic part of everyday life in Buenos Aires. *Porteños* feel cafés are almost like an extension of their home, study, or work environment. Each quarter in the city has its own trademark café, some even more than one. Each features a unique and personal style.

A busy restaurant in Buenos Aires. Traditionally, in Argentine restaurants, only men wait on tables. Waitresses are a rare sight.

In Argentina it is common for pasta to be eaten together with white bread (French bread), which is unusual in Italy. This can be explained by the low cost of bread and the fact that Argentine pasta tends to come together with a large amount of sauce and is often accompanied by *estofado* (stew).

WINE AND OTHER SPIRITS

Argentine wines are considered some of the best in South America. Argentina produces its own beer, scotch, rum, and vodka, plus some other liquors, but it exports only wine. The wines of Mendoza are much loved throughout the country. Most Argentines drink red wine with their meals. A highly prized type is called Malbec. White wines are produced in the Salta region and are also exported.

Chilean wine is also served in many restaurants in Argentina. Wine and champagne coolers mixed with fruit are popular summer drinks. A slightly alcoholic cider called *sidra* (SEE-drah) is quite popular and often substitutes for champagne on New Year's Eve. *Whiskerías* (wees-keh-REE-ahs) are numerous in Buenos Aires. These informal cocktail lounges also serve sandwiches. Generally Argentines tend to chat over coffee or a soft drink rather than cocktails. Although they love to drink wine with meals, Argentines also enjoy carbonated mineral water with their food.

A calabash gourd with its signature metal *bombilla* straw and metal pava teapot typically accompany the drinking of yerba mate.

YERBA MATE

Mate is a type of tea made from the young leaves of the Brazilian holly, an evergreen tree of the holly family. The tea leaves come both from trees grown on plantations and from trees growing wild in the Misiones jungles. Also known as Paraguayan tea, this drink is commonly called yerba mate.

To prepare it, the greenish herb is ground to the size of ordinary tea leaves. The leaves are steeped in very hot water in a gourd or bowl, then drunk from a small hole in the top through a metal straw called a *bombilla* (bohm-BEE-ya). The straw has a filter to keep the leaves out of the drinker's mouth. The bowl and the *bombilla* may be ornately decorated, often with silver. Yerba mate was developed by the indigenous Indians, adopted by the gauchos, and finally adopted by the entire country. Drinking mate in social settings, such as family gatherings or with friends, is much more common than drinking tea.

At home parties, mate may be served plain or with sugar, anise seeds, orange peel, or milk. The drink is sometimes shared socially, passed around as each person takes a sip from the same cup. Like regular tea, mate contains caffeine. In the past, the gauchos found that mate energized them so much that they could go for long stretches on horseback without food or sleep.

Beer competes with wine for popularity in Argentina. Argentines annually consume 8.8 gallons (40 liters) of beer per capita.

INTERNET LINKS

www.popular-traditional-argentina-food.com/

This site contains many yummy recipes from Argentina.

www.igourmet.com/argentinefood.asp

This site includes traditional Argentine food recipes with an option to purchase ingredients online.

http://gogreentravelgreen.com/green-restaurant-food/argentine-cuisine-17-foods-youve-gotta-try/

This site provides an online blogger's list of the 17 must-try foods in Argentina.

BIFE A CABALLO (BEEF ON HORSEBACK)

To make the *chimichurri*:

½ cup (125 ml) olive oil

¼ cup (60 ml) vinegar

1 cup (250 ml) finely chopped onion

1 teaspoon (5 ml) finely chopped or minced parsley

1 teaspoon (5 ml) dry oregano

Salt, freshly ground pepper, and ground chili peppers, to taste

- Combine all ingredients in a bowl.
- Set aside for a few hours until the flavors blend.
- Serve with cooked meat or use as a marinade before cooking.

To cook the steak:

1 beef steak (per person)

1 egg (per person)

Olive oil

Pinch of salt

- Coat each steak with olive oil and sprinkle with salt.
- Add *chimichurri* marinade.
- Grill steak to desired degree of tenderness, preferably on a charcoal grill or barbeque pit.
- Separately fry egg sunny-side up.
- When the steak is cooked, place the egg on top of the steak.
- Serve with a mixed salad, crusty bread and *chimichurri*.

DULCE DE LECHE (CARAMEL MILK JAM)

Used mainly as pastry filling, *dulce de leche* can also be enjoyed on bread. This recipe serves 10 people.

2 quarts (2 L) milk
1 pound (500 grams) sugar
½ teaspoon (2.5 ml) bicarbonate of soda
Few drops vanilla flavoring

- Heat milk in a pot until it comes to a boil.
- Remove milk from heat and transfer to a large saucepan.
- Add sugar, soda, and vanilla and continue to cook over medium heat while stirring with a wooden spoon.
- Bring the mixture to a boil and keep the temperature high. Once it boils, the sugar will begin to thicken, so keep stirring to prevent the mixture from sticking to the bottom of the pan.
- Once the mixture has thickened to the consistency of a light cream sauce, remove the pan from the heat.
- Cool the pan by placing it in a basin filled with cold water. Stir the contents until they cool. If the mixture separates, blend it until it re-forms.
- *Dulce* can be refrigerated until served.

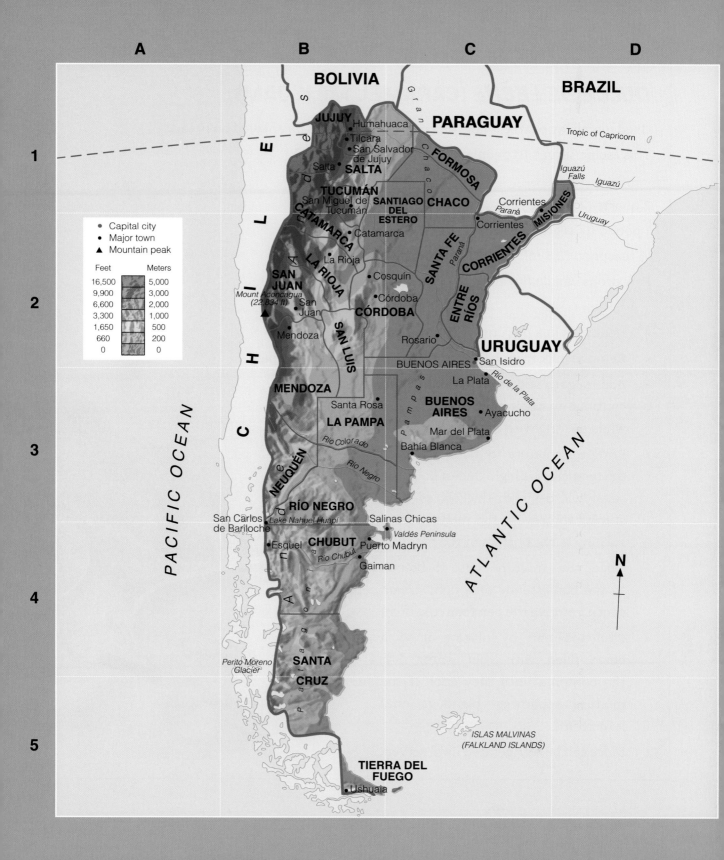

A **B** **C** **D**

BOLIVIA

BRAZIL

PARAGUAY

1

JUJUY
• Humahuaca
• Tilcara
• San Salvador
de Jujuy
• Salta SALTA

Tropic of Capricorn

FORMOSA

Iguazú
Falls   Iguazú

TUCUMÁN
San Miguel de
Tucumán

SANTIAGO
DEL
ESTERO

CHACO

Corrientes
Paraná

Corrientes

MISIONES

Uruguay

CATAMARCA
• Catamarca

SANTA FE

CORRIENTES

• La Rioja

LA RIOJA

Paraná

2

SAN
JUAN

• Cosquín

ENTRE
RÍOS

Mount Aconcagua
(22,834 ft)
▲ • San
Juan

• Córdoba

CÓRDOBA

SAN LUIS

URUGUAY

• Mendoza

• Rosario

BUENOS AIRES • San Isidro

• La Plata

Río de la Plata

MENDOZA

Santa Rosa

Pampas

BUENOS
AIRES • Ayacucho

LA PAMPA

• Mar del Plata

Río Colorado

• Bahía Blanca

3

Río Negro

NEUQUÉN

RÍO NEGRO

San Carlos
de Bariloche

Lake Nahuel Huapí

Salinas Chicas

Valdés Peninsula

• Esquel

CHUBUT

• Puerto Madryn

Río Chubut

• Gaiman

4

N

Perito Moreno
Glacier

SANTA

CRUZ

ISLAS MALVINAS
(FALKLAND ISLANDS)

5

TIERRA DEL
FUEGO
• Ushuaia

PACIFIC OCEAN

ATLANTIC OCEAN

A N D E S

C H I L E

Patagonia

Legend:
• Capital city
• Major town
▲ Mountain peak

Feet	Meters
16,500	5,000
9,900	3,000
6,600	2,000
3,300	1,000
1,650	500
660	200
0	0

Gran Chaco

MAP OF ARGENTINA

Andes, B1—B4
Atlantic Ocean,
    D1—D5
Ayacucho, C3

Bahía Blanca, C3
Bolivia, B1, C1
Brazil, C1, D1—D2
Buenos Aires,
    B2—B3, C2—C3
Buenos Aires
    (capital), C2

Catamarca, B1—B2
Catamarca (city),
    B2
Chaco, C1—C2
Chile, B1—B5
Chubut, B4
Córdoba, B2, C2
Córdoba (city), B2
Corrientes, C2
Corrientes (city), C2
Cosquín, B2

Entre Ríos, C2
Esquel, B4

Formosa, C1

Gaiman, B4
Gran Chaco, C1

Humahuaca, B1

Iguazú Falls, D1
Islas Malvinas
    (Falkland
    Islands), C5

Jujuy, B1

La Pampa, B3, C3
La Plata, C3
La Rioja, B2
La Rioja (city), B2
Lake Nahuel Itapi,
    B3

Mar del Plata, C3
Mendoza, B2—B3
Mendoza (city), B2
Misiones, C1—C2,
    D1—D2
Mount Aconcagua,
    B2

Neuquén, B3

Pacific Ocean,
    A1—A5, B1—B5
Pampas, C3
Paraguay, C1, D1
Paraná River,
    C2

Patagonia, B4—B5
Perito Moreno
    Glacier, B4
Puerto Madryn,
    B4

Río Chubut, B4
Río Colorado,
    B3, C3
Río de la Plata,
    C2—C3
Río Negro, B3—C3
Rosario, C2

Salinas Chicas, C4
Salta, B1—B2
Salta (city), B1
San Carlos de
    Bariloche, B3
San Isidro, C2
San Juan, B2
San Juan (city), B2
San Luis, B2—B3

San Miguel de
    Tucumán, B1
San Salvador de
    Jujuy, B1
Santa Cruz, B4—B5
Santa Fe, C2
Santa Rosa, B3
Santiago del Estero,
    B1—B2, C1—C2

Tierra del Fuego,
    B5, C5
Tilcara, B1
Tropic of Capricorn,
    A1, B1, C1, D1
Tucumán, B1—B2

Uruguay River,
    C2, D2
Ushuaia, B5

Valdés Peninsula,
    C4

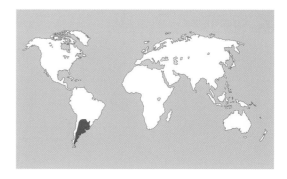

ECONOMIC ARGENTINA

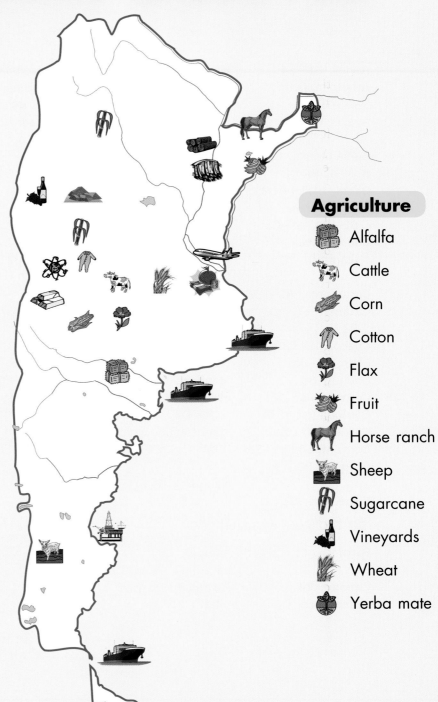

Services

 Airport

 Port

 Stock exchange

Manufacturing

 Hydroelectricity

 Iron

 Natural gas

Oil

Timber

Uranium

Agriculture

Alfalfa

Cattle

Corn

Cotton

Flax

Fruit

Horse ranch

Sheep

Sugarcane

Vineyards

Wheat

Yerba mate

ABOUT THE ECONOMY

OVERVIEW

Argentina's economic strengths lie in the nation's abundant natural resources, highly literate population, and profitable agricultural and industrial exports. The country's high inflation rates of the past few decades and a huge external debt slowed its economic growth considerably and the economy bottomed out in 2002 with almost 60 percent of Argentines below the poverty line. Real GDP rebounded and grew by an average 8.5 percent annually over the subsequent 6 years through utilization of the previously idle industrial capacity and labor, an audacious debt restructuring and reduced debt burden, excellent international financial conditions, and expansionary monetary and fiscal policies. The economy has rebounded from the 2009 recession, but the government's continued reliance on expansionary fiscal and monetary policies risks exacerbating the already high inflation.

GDP

$596 billion (2010 estimate)

GDP PER CAPITA

$14,700 (2010 estimate)

CURRENCY

1 peso = 100 centavos
$1 = 4.08 Argentine pesos (2011 estimate)

GDP SECTORS

Agriculture: 8.6 percent
Industry: 31.6 percent
Services: 59.8 percent (2010 estimate)

WORKFORCE

20 million (2010 estimate)

UNEMPLOYMENT RATE

7.9 percent (2010 estimate)

MAIN IMPORTS

Machinery, motor vehicles, petroleum and natural gas, organic chemicals, and plastics

MAIN EXPORTS

Soybeans and derivatives, petroleum and gas, vehicles, corn, and wheat

MAIN TRADING PARTNERS

Brazil, United States, China, Chile, and Germany

AGRICULTURAL PRODUCTS

Soybean, corn, sugarcane, wheat, sunflower seeds, sorghum, grapes, potatoes, lemons, and barley

TRANSPORTATION

Highways: 143,000 miles (230,137 km), of which 44,768 miles (72,047 km) are paved
Railways: 19,823 miles (31,902 km)
Airports: 1,272, of which 154 have paved runways
Main ports: Bahia Blanca, Buenos Aires, Comodoro Rivadavia, La Plata, Mar del Plata, Necochea, Rio Gallegos, Rosario, Santa Fe, and Ushuaia

CULTURAL ARGENTINA

Iguazú Falls
Located on the border between Argentina and Brazil, the horseshoe-shaped falls are 270 feet (82 m) high and 2.5 miles (4 km) wide.

Wichí Indians
Descendants of an indigenous group in Argentina continue their traditional lifestyle in the Gran Chaco region.

Yerba Mate Festival
A festival is held here every year to celebrate the mate harvest and yerba mate, Argentina's national drink.

Colonial Architecture
One of the first cities founded by the Spaniards on Argentine soil, today Córdoba is home to beautiful colonial churches and estancias.

Carnival Festivities
The lively Carnival celebrations in Corrientes, which include parades, dances, and special foods, are the most famous in Argentina.

Teatro Colón
Latin America's most lavish and prominent opera house, the theater was officially opened in 1908.

Vendimia Festival
This festival celebrates the grape harvest in Mendoza, Argentina's prime wine country.

Lake Nahuel Huapi: Perito Moreno Glacier
Located in Los Glaciares Nature Reserve in Santa Cruz Province, it is 3 miles (5 km) long and 197 feet (60 m) high.

The Pampas and the gaucho tradition
Vast, fertile lands where cattle are raised. Argentina's epic poem, *Martín Fierro*, tells the story of a gaucho's life in the Pampas.

Annual Fishing Competition
Professional and amateur fishermen gather here to try and catch the biggest trout.

Hometown of racing great Juan Fangio
Juan Fangio's museum houses the Grand Prix champion's trophies and other personal memorabilia.

Annual Welsh Singing Festival
A lively festival that was started by the descendants of Welsh immigrants in the 1800s.

Peninsula Valdés Nature Reserve and World Heritage Site
Home to rare animal species, such as the southern elephant seal and right whale.

Cave of the Hands
Prehistoric rock paintings representing hands, human figures, and guanacos are found along the valley of the Rio Pinturas.

ABOUT THE CULTURE

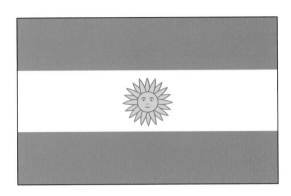

OFFICIAL NAME
República Argentina or Republic of Argentina

CAPITAL
Buenos Aires

DESCRIPTION OF FLAG
Three horizontal bands of light blue, white, and light blue with a radiant sun (Sun of May), in the middle of the white band

NATIONAL ANTHEM
Oid mortales el grito sagrado ("Listen, o mortals, the sacred cry")

POLITICS
Cristina Fernández de Kirchner, president since December 10, 2007
Voting age: 18
Constitution: Established May 1853 (last revised August 1994)

POPULATION
41.8 million (2011 estimate)

BIRTHRATE
17.75 births per 1,000 people (2011 estimate)

LIFE EXPECTANCY
Male: 73.52 years
Female: 80.17

ETHNIC GROUPS
Caucasian: 97 percent
Mestizo, Amerindian, and others: 3 percent

LITERACY RATE
Total population: 97.2 percent
Male: 97.2 percent
Female: 97.2 percent

NATIONAL HOLIDAYS
January 1—New Year's Day; January 6—Epiphany; March/April—Maundy Thursday, Good Friday, Easter Sunday; May 1—Labor Day; May 25—Anniversary of Revolution of 1810; April 2—Malvinas Day; June 20—Flag Day; July 9—Independence Day; August 17—Death of General José de San Martín; October 12—Columbus Day; December 8—Immaculate Conception; December 25—Christmas

LEADERS IN SPORTS
Diego Armando Maradona, soccer player; Gabriel Batistuta, soccer player; Lionel Messi, soccer player; Guillermo Vilas, tennis player; Gabriela Sabatini, tennis player; Franco Squillari, tennis player

LEADERS IN THE ARTS
Jorge Luis Borges, writer; Carlos Gardel, tango singer; Astor Piazzolla, tango musician; Benito Quinquela, painter; Norma Aleandro, actress

TIME LINE

IN ARGENTINA	IN THE WORLD
7,370 B.C. First hand paintings made at the Cave of the Hands in Santa Cruz province	**753 B.C.** Rome founded
1516 Juan Díaz de Solís claims Rio de la Plata for Spain.	**600 A.D.** Height of Mayan civilization
1527 Sebastian Cabot founds the first European settlement near Rosario.	**1530** Beginning of transatlantic slave trade organized by Portuguese in Africa
1536 First founding of Santa María del Buen Aire	**1558–1603** Reign of Elizabeth I of England
1580 Founding of Buenos Aires after failed attempts	
1776 Spanish Crown establishes the Viceroyalty of Rio de la Plata.	**1776** U. S. Declaration of Independence
1806–1807 Great Britain attempts to invade Buenos Aires.	**1789–1799** The French Revolution
1810 Rio de la Plata declares its independence from Spain.	
1816 Formal declaration of independence in Tucumán	
1828–1829 Civil war.	
1853–1854 New constitution is created.	
1860 The country's name is changed to Argentina.	
1890–1914 Golden Age of economic expansion	**1914** World War I begins.
1944 Juan Perón becomes vice president.	
1945 Argentina declares war on Germany and Japan.	**1945** The United States drops atomic bombs on Hiroshima and Nagasaki.
1947 Juan Perón becomes president.	**1949** North Atlantic Treaty Organization (NATO) is formed.
1955 The army and navy rebel and Juan Perón flees.	

IN ARGENTINA	IN THE WORLD
1973 Juan Perón elected president.	
1974 Perón dies. His wife, Isabel, who had been vice president, becomes president.	
1976–1983 The "dirty war"; the Falklands War started with the United Kingdom in 1982. Democratic government returns in 1983 where Raúl Alfonsín becomes president.	**1986** Nuclear power disaster at Chernobyl in Ukraine **1991** Breakup of Soviet Union
1999 Fernando de la Rúa is elected president.	**1997** Hong Kong is returned to China.
2000 Strikes and fuel tax protests. The IMF grants Argentina an aid package of nearly $40 billion.	
2001 Opposition Perónists take control of both houses of parliament in congressional elections. President Fernando de la Rúa resigns and new interim president Adolfo Rodriguez Saa resigns after a week as well.	**2001** World population surpasses 6 billion.
2002 Congress elects Perónist senator Eduardo Duhalde as caretaker president.	
2003 Néstor Kirchner is sworn in as president.	**2004** Eleven Asia countries hit by giant tsunami, killing at least 225,000 people.
2005 President Kirchner declares the restructuring of the country's debt to be a success.	
2007 Cristina Fernández de Kirchner, wife of Néstor Kirchner, is elected and sworn in as president.	**2008** Earthquake in Sichuan, China, kills 67,000 people. **2009** Outbreak of flu virus H1N1 around the world
2010 Argentina legalizes same-sex marriage; ex-President Néstor Kirchner dies.	
2011 Unofficial inflation estimates hit 25 to 30 percent.	**2011** Twin earthquake and tsunami disasters strike northeast Japan, leaving over 14,000 dead.

GLOSSARY

bandoneón (bahn-doh-NYOHN)
An instrument similar to the accordion, often used when performing the tango.

confitería (kohn-fee-teh-REE-ah)
A casual eatery found only in Argentina that serves coffee, tea, pastries, and light meals.

corralito (kor-rah-LIT-toh)
The diminutive form of *corral*, which means "corral," "animal pen," or "enclosure." The diminutive is used in the sense of "small enclosure" and also "a child's playpen."

criollo
A person of Spanish descent born in Latin America.

diarchy (DAHY-ahr-kee)
Government in which power is vested in two rulers or authorities.

estancia
A large cattle ranch.

fiestas
Festivities linked to special holidays.

gaucho
A horseman and cowboy of the pampas, usually a mestizo.

lunfardo (loon-FAR-doh)
A slang language, originally used by the criminals of Buenos Aires. It is used in tango music, popular songs, poetry, and the theater.

mestizo
Person of mixed European and Indian ancestry.

Pampas
The flat grass plains of central Argentina.

parrillada (par-ree-ZHAH-dah)
A restaurant that specializes in serving meats grilled over a charcoal fire.

pato (PAH-toh)
A sport played on horseback, in which players attempt to throw a six-handled leather ball into a net at the opposing team's end of the playing field.

peninsulares (pay-neen-soo-LAH-rehs)
Spaniards who occupied all high government positions in the Latin American colonies.

piropo (pee-ROH-poh)
A casual comment made by a man to attract a woman's attention as she passes by.

porteños (porr-TEH-nyos)
The people of the city of Buenos Aires.

tango
A dance, accompanied by music, in which a couple hold each other and take long, gliding steps together, occasionally pausing in a dramatic pose.

yerba mate
A holly tea sipped from a gourd through a metal straw.

FOR FURTHER INFORMATION

BOOKS

Dell O'ro, Suzanne Paul. *Argentina* (Country Explorers). Minneapolis, MN: Lerner Classroom, 2008.

Favor, Lesli J. *Eva Perón*. New York: Marshall Cavendish Benchmark, 2011.

Hamnwee, Robert. *Argentina—Culture Smart!: A Quick Guide to Customs & Culture*. London, United Kingdom: Kuperard, 2006.

Mattern, Joan. *Eva Peron* (The Great Hispanic Heritage). New York, NY: Chelsea House Publishers, 2010.

Whelan, Gloria. *The Disappeared*. New York, NY: Speak (Penguin), 2010.

VIDEOS

Imagining Argentina. Universal Studios, 2005.

Passport to Adventure: Buenos Aires and Bariloche Argentina. TravelVideoStore.com, 2009.

7 Days Argentina. TravelVideoStore.com, 2010.

MUSIC

En Vivo En Argentina. Silvio Rodriguez, BMG Argentina, 2008.

From Argentina to the World. Alfredo De Angelis, EMI Argentina, 2006.

The Tantalizing Tangos of Argentina. Buenos Aires Tango Orchestra, Legacy International, 2009.

WEBSITES

Diego Maradona's official Website. www.diegomaradona.com (in Spanish)

Everything an enterprising cook needs to make Argentine food. http://argentineanrecipe.com/

News about agriculture in Argentina. http://agriculture.einnews.com/argentina/

Site dedicated to the Argentines who disappeared during the 1976—1983 military regime. www.yendor.com/vanished

Tango English language site. www.abctango.com.ar (in Spanish)

Tango music site, plays tango songs. www.buenosairestango.com

Travel Guide to Argentina including Argentine culture and history. www.justargentina.org/

BIBLIOGRAPHY

BOOKS

Bao, Sandra; Clark, Gregor; Gleeson, Bridget; and Symington, Andy. *Lonely Planet Argentina* (Country Guide). Oakland, CA: Lonely Planet, 7th edition, 2010.

Benson, Andrew; and O'Brien, Rosalba. *The Rough Guide to Buenos Aires 1* (Rough Guide Travel Guides). London, UK: Rough Guides, 2008.

Cardinale, Ana; Estrada, Isabel de; Taschen, Angelika; and Labouqle, Ricardo (Illustrator). *Living in Argentina* (Taschen's Lifestyle). Los Angeles: TASCHEN America Llc, 2008.

DK Publishing. *Argentina*: *Eyewitness Travel Guide.* New York: DK Travel, 2010.

Luongo, Michael; O'Malley, Charlie; and Pashby, Christie. *Frommer's Argentina* (Frommer's Complete). Hoboken, NJ: Frommers, 2009.

WEBSITES

Argentina — Ministry of Tourism. www.turismo.gov.ar/eng/menu.htm

Geographia.com — Argentina. www.geographia.com/argentina/

Infoplease.com — Argentina. www.infoplease.com/ipa/A0107288.html

Just Argentina.org. www.justargentina.org/

Latin American Network Information Center — Argentina. http://lanic.utexas.edu/la/argentina/

Lonely Planet Argentina. www.lonelyplanet.com/argentina.

INDEX

INDEX